THE COSTS OF PLEASURE

1803

Apr. 20   Bath — Br.d over £ 113. 11. 3
          Letters 7 — Lozenges 1/2 ..... 1. 9
          Pump J. 1/6. Chair 1/ — ... " 2. 6
          Box book keeper 2/6. Ch.a 2/ ... 4. 6
          Doyle's benefit 10. 6
     21   Paid at Mollands for a } ~ 15. 8
          Fowl Pye sent v.d Dr Myd.n }
          Paid Pickwick for Post horses — 15. —
          Paid Hemming for 2 Cream }
          Cheese sent Mrs Spilsbury } ..... 4. —
          Pmp 2/400/ 2/ Chair 1/ ..... 3. —
          3 Tickets for Pizarro ..... 12. —
          Chair .... " 1. —
     22   Waiters upp.r Rooms 10. 6
          Porters at d.o .... 5. —
          Bathing 3/ waiters/ Ch.o 1/ — " 5. —
          Ch.o to Mr Temple/ ..... " 1. —
     23   Paid Wm for Sundries 5. 8
          D.o for Washing ..... " 5. 4
          Paid for 1/4 lb Fry's Cocoa — " 1. —
          Waiters Lower rooms 10. 6
          Porters at d.o ..... 5. —
          Henry to the Play ..... " 1. 6
          2 Tickets Play to Night — " 8. —
          3 for Thursday next — " 12. —
          Paid at Sayers & Co. for } 1. 16. —
          12 border'd Scotch cambric }
          Hnkfs at 3/ ..... £ 122. 7. 8

The Costs of Pleasure

VISITING GEORGIAN BATH
AND OTHER SPAS

The Family & Excursions of
Jacob & Priscilla Franks

COLIN FISHER

THE HOBNOB PRESS

First published in the United Kingdom in 2025
by The Hobnob Press,
8 Lock Warehouse, Severn Road, Gloucester GL1 2GA
www.hobnobpress.co.uk

British Library Cataloguing in Publication Data
A catalogue record for this book is available from the British Library

ISBN 978-1-914407-91-8

Typeset in Adobe Garamond Pro, 11/14 pt
Typesetting and origination by John Chandler

Front cover illustration: The Comforts of Bath, 1798, by Thomas Rowlandson (Bath in Time).
Back cover: West front of the Abbey Church, Bath 1788, aquatint by Thomas Malton (Bath in Time).

CONTENTS

A GUIDE TO
EIGHTEENTH-CENTURY MONEY

Denominations

4 farthings = 1 penny
2 halfpennies = 1 penny
12 pennies = 1 shilling   = 5p   in decimal currency
20 shillings = 1 pound   = 100p   in decimal currency
Written as £ -s –d, or for just shillings and pence 2/6
The Georgians often abbreviated pounds with an italicised letter 'l' as a suffix,
    for example, 6L.
1 pound and 1 shilling = a guinea   = £1.05p   in decimal currency
2 shillings and 6 pence = a half a crown

Modern equivalent values:
£1 in 1780 is equivalent to £86-10d in 2017 values;
or equal to 6 days of a skilled tradesman's wages in 1780
1 shilling = £4. 31p in 2017 values.
£1 in 1810 is equivalent to £46-53d in 2017 values;
or equal to 6 days of a skilled tradesman's wages in 1810,
1 shilling = £2-33p in 2017 values.
    (National Archives Historical Currency Converter)

1 pagoda (gold) = 42 fanams (silver) = 80 cash (copper) = 8 shillings 9 pence
    in Calcutta in 1799.

PLEASE NOTE

THE BOOK INCLUDES quotations from historical documents that include derogatory vocabulary used at the time and which also exhibit racist, anti-Semitic and other prejudicial attitudes that were then widely accepted, though not without contemporary challenge. There are description of the treatment, and attitudes towards, enslaved people on West Indian plantations.

Much of this book is based on entries in cash account books that are brief, abbreviated and sometimes obscure because they only had to mean something to the book keeper. Interpreting them requires research aided by ingenuity and epiphanies and so inevitably, sometimes, I will have got things wrong; I will always be happy to be corrected.

Colin Fisher

I
INTRODUCTION

JANE AUSTEN'S DESCRIPTIONS in *Persuasion* and *Northanger Abbey* of stays in Bath include walks, paying visits, coffee shops and balls at the Assembly Rooms. How well does this tally with the actual experiences of the well-off and gentlemanly people who visited contemporaneously with Austen's characters? What about the practicalities of a visit to Bath? How wealthy did people have to be to enjoy the pleasures of the city? What were the costs of the mundane quotidian tasks that had to be undertaken during a visit to the city such as renting lodgings, getting the coach repaired, hiring extra chairs and a caterer for a card party, paying tips to the waiters, buying clothes for the servants and negotiating fares with the sedan chairmen? How did a visit to Bath compare with other spas and resorts? In the London Metropolitan Archives there is a cash book[1] that records a couple's everyday activities and expenditures whilst they were visiting Bath and other spas; there is another cash book that covers some of the expenses while travelling between these resorts and their home.[2] These account books help answer these questions about costs and make it possible to recreate how such visitors to the city amused themselves, what they shopped for, what they ate and drank and the practical issues of everyday life.

The couple were Jacob (as a young man sometimes known as John) and Priscilla Franks who were second cousins from a wealthy Anglo-Jewish-American family; they were married to each other and were frequent visitors to Bath; visiting the city at least eight times between 1777 and 1808. Bath in the last quarter of the eighteenth century was still the fashionable resort it

---

1   Account Book chiefly expenses incurred during a residence in Bath; possibly belonging to Priscilla Franks, 1777-1808. Cooper, Honywood and Dawkins papers, London Metropolitan Archives, ref . Acc/0775/071. The cash book has no page numbers and so references to it are made by using the dates of the entries in the book.

2   Travelling Expenses cash book, London Metropolitan Archives, ref. Acc/0775/0713.

had been since the start of the century, however the Franks, along with other fashionable tourists, were also attracted to alternative spas, seaside bathing, tours of stately houses, picturesque ruins and inspecting the locations of the industrial revolution's manufacturing and transport innovations; and so visits to Bath were interspersed with such other outings.

Many diaries survive that describe daily life in Georgian and Regency Bath but they are selective, recording what the diarists wished to remember or in some case, wanted future readers to know of them. Cash books are different because they are exhaustive recording everything people did because everything in those times required expenditure, whether purchase, subscription, rental, commissions or tips. The entries are often terse because the writer knew what they referred to and some resemble cryptic crossword clues. Often these can be solved by reference to dictionaries and the historical context: inevitably some of these solutions may prove wrong. What a cash book does not reveal so easily, that a diary would, are social contacts and friendships. Nevertheless many people the Franks met with are named in the book and they are, apart from tradesmen and servants, like Mr Temple in Bath and Mr Lascelles in Yorkshire from wealthy and socially prominent land owning families, suggesting that Jacob and Priscilla had an entrée to polite society. They were sufficiently sociable to have elaborately decorated visiting cards made.[3] They also had wide family connections and Jacob in particular was remembered as an amiable man.

The writer and keeper of the cash book, whether Jacob or Priscilla, is not directly identified.[4] Normally household and daily expenditure was the province of the mistress of the household but references in the book to 'Mrs F' and 'self' suggest it may have been Jacob's book. The cash book does seem however to cover both of their activities and expenditures while in Bath and elsewhere. There was money spent on shooting and gunsmiths as well as purchases of expensive textiles which implies without being two presumptuous about eighteenth century gender roles that both Jacob's and Priscilla's activities were recorded. As the cash book covers a long period of time it allows a perspective on how the couple's habits during visits to Bath changed over the years, as they got older, their wider family became more established in the city and, perhaps as the attraction of the city to fashionable society and the 'ton' changed.

3   The Franks' Visiting Cards, British Museum, C,1.1183-1197

4   Brown, M. & Samuel, J. (1986)) 'The Jews of Bath', *Jewish Historical Studies*, Vol. 29, pp. 135-164. On p.150 it states that the cash book was Jacob's but the London Metropolitan Archives's catalogue describes the book as 'probably Priscilla Franks'.

The costs of a visit to Bath were not restricted to the direct expenses of families like the Franks, there were also costs to the people and places from where and from whom the Franks and others like them drew their wealth. There are further documents in the London Metropolitan Archives that, together with other records and published historical research, allow the sources of the Franks' wealth, the wherewithal that funded their visits to Bath, to be found. It mostly came from British colonial trade, including the importation of diamonds from India and furs from America, land speculation in America, sugar plantations in the West Indies, exporting ginseng to China, and by supplying the British army in America. The profitability of these trades often depended on leveraging colonial power to the disadvantage of the local or indigenous peoples. In particular the sources give a detailed insight into Jacob Franks' dealings with his sugar plantation in Jamaica. The leisured life and pleasures of the Franks can be contextualised by the money that paid for it.

2

THE FRANKS FAMILY AND OTHER JEWISH
VISITORS TO BATH

THE SUCCESS OF Bath as a fashionable resort in the late eighteenth century was partly the result of the openness of its social elite; if you dressed and behaved as a gentleman the Assembly Rooms would be open to you. Wealthy Jews were accordingly accepted in the company.

Jews from propertied merchant families were frequent visitors to Bath in the eighteenth century.[5] Several Jewish merchants including Mr Diaz, Marcus Moses and Joseph Musaphie were on the first subscription list in 1721 for the building of a General Hospital in Bath. Catherine da Costa was another early Jewish visitor to the city; she went there with her children in 1731 to convalesce after an illness. One of her daughters Sarah Mendes da Costa married Ephraim Lopes Pereira d'Aguilar (1739-1802), a baron of the Holy Roman Empire, and so she became Baroness d'Aguilar and was the senior lady at two balls in the Bath Assembly Rooms in May 1760.[6] One of the Baronesses' daughters was Leah d'Aguilar who married Raphael Franco a wealthy London diamond merchant; he was also an acquaintance of the Franks family and was one of the executors of Priscilla's father's will.

The Franks' Visiting cards: permission of the Trustees of the British Museum.

5   Brown,Malcolm & Samuel, Judith op cit.

6   *Bath Journal,* 5th & 12th May 1760.

The Franco's were regular visitors to Bath. On the 7th January 1775 a Miss Franco reserved a box in the Theatre Royal in Orchard Street to see a play and on the 14th February she reserved three boxes, including one for Mrs Franco, in the tier of boxes named for King Alfred (each tier was allocated a king's name), to see 'The Choleric Man' and 'The Chaplet'[7](See illustration on p. 58). Leah Franco, Raphael's wife, died at Belmont in the city in 1816.

Many of those who came to Bath did so for their health and in consequence there were many doctors in the city including a few 'Jew Doctors'. One of them, Ralph [Raphael] Schomberg had been brought up a Jew but had converted to Anglicanism; he practised in Bath until the 1770s.[8] He was on the receiving end of some prejudice and was accused in 1778 by Philip Thicknesse, a noted quarrelsome and spiteful character, of pilfering from his own offertory plate at the door of his church. A caricature published in London titled 'Brothers in Iniquity' showed Schomberg holding the offertory plate with a horned devil whispering in his ear. However Thicknesse was equally lampooned with a dog urinating on one of his books and the caricature implied that both Schomberg and Thicknesse were equally lacking in virtue. Schomberg had never finished his medical education at the University of Giessen in Hesse in Germany, having been expelled because of bad debts, and he finally gained his MD by correspondence from Marischall College in Aberdeen.

Dr Philip De la Cour who also practised in Bath from premises in Princess Street was probably better qualified having completed his medical training at Leyden. He had been born in London in 1710 as Abraham Gomez Ergaz, the son of Portuguese Jewish refugees.

Acceptance within Bath's polite society did not mean an absence of anti-Semitic feeling. On one visit on the 13th March 1780 Raphael Franco met Edmund Rack in the Assembly Rooms and Rack's remarks about him[9] reveal an atavistic prejudice;

7   Theatre Royal, Box keeper's book, (1774-1775), Bath Record Office, Local Studies Collection, BAT/30/1.

8   Courtney, W P revised Samuel, E. (2004) 'Ralph Schomberg', *Oxford Dictionary of National Biography*, Oxford University Press, 2004; online edn . Brothers in iniquity, Jewish Museum, London, available on the World Wide Web at URL http://www.jewishmuseum.org.uk/?unique_name=search-our-collections-new&adlibid=5722.

9   Rack, Edmund, *A Disultory Journal of Events in Bath*, 1779-1780, online typescript, https://www.batharchives.co.uk/explore-our-online-exhibition; manuscript, Mss. 1.112; RAC/1/1-3, Bath Record Office.

went to the Rooms and persuaded Franco, the great Jew who had lately four hundred thousand pounds left to him by the death of his father, to become a member of the Bath [philosophical & literary] Society. He is about 4 foot 7 inches high, made all askew, with legs like ninepins, an eye like a hawk & a nose form'd like a quadrant. His mouth is very wide, his ears remarkably long, and the end of his chin turn'd up like a bent potatoe. His voice is like Nat Brays, and he turns half round every step he walks. Yet this some thing like nothing has got near half a million of money. Certainly all things are not quite right in this world at least.

Brothers in Iniquity: courtesy of the Jewish Museum, London

Perhaps this envy resulted from Rack's own difficult climb from being a shop keeper to being accepted within Bath society. The idea that Jews were not polite company was common. Amabel Hume-Campbell wrote to her sister from Tunbridge Wells during the summer season of 1775:[10]

> Tuesday, Ld P [Lord Polworth her husband] ventured to the Dress'd Ball having engag'd with Mrs Acheson to dance but two dances & is not the worst of it – I ought not to say much of so unchristian a Party, unchristian I repeat for believe me half of the Room were Jews, two Jew Children made one of the Couples, [ ] – to be short, the undress'd Balls are to be the only genteel and fashionable ones.

She had attended an 'undressed ball' earlier in the week and had found the company acceptable. Jacob and Priscilla Franks however assimilated relatively easily into the English gentry and Bath's society.

Bath's acceptance of Jacob and Priscilla Franks was eased not only by their wealth but by their adoption of English habits and Anglicanism. The Franks family originated in Hanover, Germany but had come to England

---

10   Letter of Amabel Hume-Campbell, Bedfordshire Archives and Record Service, Wrest Park (Lucas) Mss, L30/13/12/27.

when the Hanoverians became the British royal family. Some such as Jacob's grandfather, also called Jacob Franks, had emigrated from England to America at the start of the eighteenth century and he became an eminent citizen of New York working in the shipping, privateering and slave trading businesses. In New York Jacob married Bilhal Abigail Levy the daughter of the leading Jewish merchant in the city at that time. The couple had three sons, Naphtali (Heartsey), Moses and David, and two daughters Phila and Rachel.

Jacob Franks junior, Priscilla's husband, was the son of the youngest of the three brothers David Franks who was born in New York in 1720. His brothers Naphtali and Moses both married Jewish women but David married a non-Jew, Margaret Evans, in Philadelphia in 1743; she was the daughter of another Philadelphian merchant. David's mother Abigail, although widely read in enlightenment literature, was very conservative when it came to the observance of Jewish custom and was deeply unhappy that David had married out of the faith, but could not bring herself to break with him entirely. (When her daughter Phila also married a non-Jew Abigail did break with her). David Franks led a dual religious life; in Philadelphia he would attend church on a Sunday and when he was with his family in New York he would attend synagogue.[11] So by this time the Franks family were in part already assimilating into Anglican society. After two generations all Jacob senior and Abigail's descendants had converted to Christianity. Like his father David Franks was a merchant and financial broker working as a member of the wider Franks' family business.

Jacob Franks, David's son, was born on the 7th January 1747 and was baptised on the 20th April 1747.[12] Some at least, if not all, of his siblings were also baptised at various times. When he was eighteen Jacob moved to Britain and probably not long after his arrival he married his cousin Priscilla Franks,[13] a union that had likely been planned before he left Philadelphia. Her sister Phila Franks had married Jacob's uncle Moses in 1765 and Phila and Moses lived at Teddington on the River Thames[14] near to Priscilla's father's home at Isleworth.

11   Stern, Mark Abbott (2010), *David Franks, Colonial Merchant*, Pennsylvania State University p. 15.

12   Stern, op cit, cithg Hildeburn, C.R. *Records of Christ Church, Philadelphia.*

13   Stern op cit p.92.

14   Daiches-Dubens, Rachel (1953-1955) 'Eighteenth Century Anglo-Jewry in and around Richmond, Surrey', *Transactions (Jewish History Society of England)* Vol. 18,pp. 143-55, Finberg, Hilda, F. (1945-1951) 'Jewish Residents in Eighteenth Century Twickenham', *Transactions (Jewish History Society of England)* Vol. 16, pp. 129-135. Stern, M. H. (1991) *First American Jewish Families*, Ottenheimer

Priscilla was born in about 1747; her sister Phila was a year older.[15] They were the daughters of Aaron Franks a hugely wealthy diamond merchant of Billeter Square in the city of London. Their mother was Bilah Hart the daughter of Moses Hart an influential and wealthy stock broker and banker who dealt in Government and East India Company stock. Bilah and Aaron Franks were married in 1743 and Bilah died six years later in 1749. In a court case in 1757 in a dispute over the will of Moses Hart who had died in 1756 Priscilla and Phila Franks' aunt Abigail Salomons was named as their Guardian[16] even though their father was still alive. Perhaps as young girls they lived with their widowed aunt after their mother's death.

Priscilla's father Aaron Franks had been born in London in 1692 where his father Jacob was a financial broker and merchant. Despite being Jewish Aaron Franks managed to gain a degree of acceptance by the wealthy

Priscilla Franks by Reynolds

and noble neighbouring families of Richmond and Twickenham. He was an acquaintance of Horace Walpole of Strawberry Hill who spoke of the splendid entertainments he had received at Isleworth House, and gossiped that Franks had once loaned £40,000 worth of jewels to the Princess of Wales for a ball 'only desiring that she would tell whose they were'. Franks was also a great philanthropist and was familiar with Bath being one of the second round of subscribers to the Bath General Hospital [Royal Mineral Water Hospital] in the city. Aaron Franks died in 1777.

Publications Baltimore p. 75.

15 In a submission to the Court of Chancery in 1757 Phila was said to be eleven years old and Priscilla ten years old and they were both the daughters of Aaron and Bilah Franks. Franks v Adolphus, National Archives, C/11/1683/21.

16 *House of Lord's Journal*, Vol. 29: March, 1760, 11-20, British History Online; Brown, J. (1757) *Reports of Cases upon Appeal & Writs of Error in the High Court of Parliament*, Vol. 5, marriage and death of Bilah Hart/Franks, p.423. In his will Moses Hart did not make provision for Phila and Priscilla because their father was also wealthy and possessed of large estates however in a codicil he did express great love and respect for them, p. 425.

Reynolds painted portraits of Priscilla and her sister in 1766 before the latter's marriage; the whereabouts of Priscilla's portrait is unknown but an early twentieth century photograph of it exists.[17] After her marriage Priscilla's father Aaron tried to bring his son-in-law back to Judaism and he purchased the couple a membership of the Great Synagogue in London for 1767-8 but when it expired after a year the couple did not renew it and instead attended All Saints parish church in Isleworth.

The wider Franks family of Richmond and Isleworth assimilated into English upper class Anglican society, but not all. Naphtali (Heartsey) Franks (d.1796), Jacob's uncle, although broadly accepted into polite English society and a fellow of the Royal Society, did not convert to Anglicanism but remained a practising Jew and a leading member of the London Jewish community. Daiches-Dubens[18] suggests that one reason many of the Richmond Franks integrated was because as Ashkenazi Jews they were a marginal family amongst the Sephardic dominated London Jewish society; and assimilation was also a way to integrate with Richmond's gentry society. It also most likely eased their entry to polite society and the Assembly Rooms at Bath.

Aaron, Jacob and Priscilla Franks' family home Isleworth House was burgled in 1773. Aaron Franks was away but Jacob, and probably Priscilla, were at home. Five guineas, two pounds in cash in a leather bag, a gold watch and chain, cornelian seals, pinchbeck gilt waistcoat buttons and a quantity of clothing were stolen from Jacob's dressing room but the burglars and fences were caught and tried at the Old Bailey.[19] The thieves' swag shows that the Franks were wealthy and lived in comfort at Isleworth. Some surviving visiting cards from the 1780s show that Priscilla, Mrs J Franks of Isleworth, and probably Jacob as well also stayed at a house in Great George Street in Westminster, a prestigious address, that belonged to Naphtali Franks, who was Priscilla's cousin as well as Jacob's uncle. The house, No.31, was part of a private speculative housing development begun by James Mallors in the 1750s.[20] Naphtali was the first tenant of the 'good and substantial' house after

17   Ruben, Alfred (1955-1959) 'Portrait of Anglo-Jewry, 1656-1836', *Transactions (Jewish History Society of England)* Vol. 19 pp.13-52, p.24 and plate no. 20. The last known location of the portrait was at an Exhibition in Birmingham in 1903.

18   Daiches-Dubens op cit.

19   Old Bailey Proceedings: Accounts of Criminal Trials, 9/91772, available online at LondonLives.org/.browse.jsp?id=t177207.

20   Cox, M. H. (1926) *Survey of London*, Vol. 10, pt. 1, St Margaret's Westminster, pp51-52. Available online at British History Online, & Garneir, R. (2002) 'Speculative Housing in 1750's London', *The Georgian Group Journal*, Vol.XII, p.165.

it was completed in 1761 and in 1765 he bought the property. (The Mr Franks of the visiting cards was probably Naphtali rather than Jacob).It remained in the Franks family, although let out to tenants from 1786 onwards, until 1803 when Naphtali's son Jacob Henry Franks sold it. No. 31 was obviously used by the wider Franks family including Jacob and Priscilla as a London base; and of course the couple were sufficiently well-off to be able to spend seasons in Bath and to take tours around Britain; holidays that are explored in the rest of this book.

Isleworth house

3
THE PLEASURES OF BATH: WINTER
SEASON, 1777

THE FRANKS' FIRST visit to Bath recorded in the cash book was for the winter season of 1777. This was not their first visit to the city. The 'arrivals' section of the *Bath Chronicle* and the *Bath Journal* record other visits by a Mr & Mrs Franks and although it cannot be certain that these always referred to Jacob and Priscilla it is highly probable that most did. The first occasion on which Mr & Mrs Franks are noted was in November 1766 so this would have been not long after their marriage and they returned for the winter season in the city a year later. There were no visits between 1767 and 1771 but in 1772 the arrival of Mr & Mrs and three misses Franks was reported. Assuming this was Jacob and Priscilla two of the three Misses can be surmised to be their nieces Charlotte Franks and Abigail Franks (b.1754) the unmarried daughters of Naphtali (Heartsey) Franks. Priscilla and Jacob would have known the girls well from their visits to Naphtali's house in Great George Street, Westminster. The third 'Miss' may have been Jacob's sister Abigail. This visit was followed by a regular pattern of annual visits to Bath by Priscilla and Jacob for either the spring or the winter season until the November visit in 1777 when they had with them the cash book in which they recorded their expenditure in the city.

One disadvantage of using a cash book as a source of information is that although it reveals what the Franks did and what they spent their money on it does not tell us who was in their party visiting Bath; however there are enough clues to make some surmises. As the Franks paid 2 guineas for the subscription to Mr LaMotte's concert at the Lower Assembly Rooms this suggests, as the price was a guinea for gentlemen and ½ guinea for ladies, that the party was Jacob, Priscilla and another woman. This other woman was almost certainly Jacob's niece 'Abby', Abigail, Franks who, as we have seen, had previously accompanied Jacob and Priscilla on a trip to Bath. During this second visit Jacob and Priscilla bought her a pearl pin. A 'great coat for J.D' and 'a waistcoat for J.D'A' were also purchased; possibly a reference to the d'Aguilar family, who have been already mentioned, and were another wealthy Jewish merchant family who are known to have visited Bath, but whether d'Aguilar was actually one of the party is unknown.

The Franks brought their own servants with them and the accounts mention paying a 'Tom's bills' and travelling expenses, he was probably one of the servants, other servants mentioned are John, Clarke who was paid for doing the laundry and Sam who was paid for household expenses.

THE PLACES OF RESORT IN BATH

When Jacob and Priscilla Franks visited Bath the main places of public resort were the Pump Room, the Lower, long established, Assembly Rooms, the New or Upper Assembly Rooms, the Theatre Royal, libraries, coffee shops, the Abbey and the parish churches. The Pump Room had been built 1704-6 and enlarged in 1751 and was a place to drink the waters and socialise. The three, allegedly health giving, hot mineral water springs in the city were the foundation of Bath's status as a resort and spa. There were subscriptions to be paid to the Assembly Rooms where the balls, concerts and ridottos were held. The Lower Rooms that had been operating since the early eighteenth century were known by the Franks' time as Gyde's Rooms after their proprietor Cam Gyde.

Gyde's Rooms seen from North Parade 1779: courtesy of Akeman Press.

The New or Upper Assembly Rooms that had opened in 1771 were designed by John Wood the Younger and paid for by subscribers drawn from country gentry and the wealthier Bath citizens. Until 1777 the two Assembly Rooms shared a Master of Ceremonies but after a dispute between them they opted each to have its own Master of Ceremonies, which was the situation when the Franks arrived.

The new, Upper, Assembly Rooms: courtesy of Akeman Press.

During the Franks' first visit to Bath the Guildhall was still being built; its grand Banqueting Room was designed to give the city corporation, whose members were often tradesmen (albeit well-off) and so socially excluded from the Assembly Rooms, a place to hold their own sumptuous entertainments.[21] (Although many of the original shareholders who invested in the building of the New Assembly Rooms were Bath merchants and property developers). The theatre was in Orchard Street and had held its first performance in 1750 and in 1768 it was granted a Royal licence and became the Theatre Royal. It was remodelled in 1766 and all the great actors of the eighteenth century performed there. There were many coffee shops in the city, the best of which such as Mr Frappell's in Orange Grove required a subscription and there were proprietary chapels which also used subscriptions as a means of excluding the lower social orders.

The Franks rented a house at Milsom Street for 5 guineas a week on their arrival. The next day they paid the ½ guinea (10/6d) subscription for the Lower Assembly Rooms, which permitted general admission to the Rooms, and then the guinea subscription to attend the weekly Dress Balls. The following day at the New Rooms they paid their subscriptions for general admittance and the Dress Balls, for the same fee as those in the Lower Rooms. One advantage of admittance to the Rooms during the winter season was

21   Forsyth, Michael (2003) *Bath*, Pevsner Architectural Guides, p.76. For example Francis Bennett was a Bath linen draper who was also a councilman and was twice Mayor; he was one of the Committee who signed off Baldwin's plans and elevations for the Guildhall but he was also one of the original shareholders who paid for the New Assembly Rooms to be built.

Milsom Street: author's collection

that, as Philip Thicknesse pointed out in his 1778 guide to Bath, 'the Public Rooms are constantly kept open, warmed by good fires, and lighted up at Great Expence for the Reception of the Company'.[22]

The Franks also paid the ½ guinea subscription to attend the 'Cotillion Balls' at the Upper Rooms as well as 5/- for the 'Ringers', this final subscription paid for the peal of church bells that was often rung to announce a family's arrival at Bath.[23] The first Cotillion Ball of the season at the Upper Rooms had been held on the Thursday 17th October, before the Franks had arrived in the city, and they continued on subsequent Thursdays. The Cotillion was a French country square dance involving four partners that had become popular in the 1760s. These balls were probably less formal than the Dress Balls at which the intricate and stately minuet was danced in the first part of the evening, with couples (or in later years pairs of couples) taking it in turns to dance while scrutinised by the on-looking assembly. Only then after the refreshment break could people enjoy the boisterous country dances. The Dress Balls at the New Rooms were held on Monday evenings and the first had been on the 13th October. The Franks would seem to have enjoyed the Cotillion Balls

22   Thicknesse, P. (1778) 2nd ed. *The New Prose Guide to Bath for the Year 1778*, p.10.

23   Fawcett, Trevor (1998) *Bath Entertain'd: Amusements, Recreations, and Gambling in the Eighteenth century Spa,* Bath, Ruton Press., p. 14.

best because in their second week in Bath they paid the subscription for the Cotillion Balls in the Lower Rooms. The Franks also went to a 'Sharpers Ball' on the 14th November (the cost was 'ball, chair and tea 7/6d') and another ball on the 12th December, the entry reads 'ball & chair 2/6d Fontaine 10/6d: -13s -0'. Perhaps the half a guinea was paid to Mr Fontaine the French dancing master to teach the Franks the cotillion or the new minuet called 'L'Intelligence des Dames'. Two years later Mr Fontaine was in Dublin advertising his services teaching varied dances to 'Ladies and gentlemen of distinction' and announcing that he had previously taught dancing at Spa, London and Bath. So it is not improbable that he taught Jacob and Priscilla.[24] The ball in December and the one in November were both held on a Friday which seems to have been an evening when there were no public balls in either of the Assembly Rooms so probably these were two of the many private parties that were held during the season at Bath. It is unclear what a Sharpers Ball was, one possibility is that it was a satirical name coined by Jacob for a masquerade because it was commonly said that such masked balls meant that undesirable people such as card sharpers, gamblers and cheats, could infiltrate the event.

There were two balls in the Assembly Rooms that were particularly grand and important and these were the Benefit Balls for the Masters of Ceremonies at each of the Rooms. Priscilla and Jacob Franks bought their tickets for the ball for Mr Brereton Master of Ceremonies at the Lower Rooms on the 15th December and the event took place on the 19th. The tickets for Mr Dawson's Benefit at the New Rooms were bought on Christmas Day and the Ball was on the 29th. Social rank was important at the formal balls; on the 5th November as the Franks arrived at Bath Mr Dawson of the New Rooms published a reminder in the Chronicle that 'the first two rows of the sophas at the top end of the ball room are reserved for Ladies of the rank of Peeresses of Great Britain and Ireland' and he 'humbly requested that no lady beneath that degree of precedence will take up any of the seats on ball nights'. Seating would have been helpful on evenings when the ballroom was crowded and over-heated with peers, baronets, officers, gentlemen, nabobs, (who had returned from India with their fortunes), wives, daughters and independent women. As Philip Francis who had been a senior East India Company official wrote to a friend 'What with the Indians [nabobs] and the heat, in the [Assembly] Rooms I mean, I fancy myself happily in Calcutta'.[25]

---

24   *Dublin Evening Post*, 7/12/1779, p.2b. Fontaine remained in Dublin and taught dancing for over twenty years until his death in the city in 1803, *Oracle & Daily Advertiser* 12/11/1803, p.4c.

25   Letter by Philip Francis, a postscript dated 1st January 1790 to a letter dated

TAKING REFRESHMENTS IN ASSEMBLY ROOM BALLS

The Assembly Rooms Managing Committee wanted to provide a top quality supper for the opening Ridotto of the New Rooms in Bath on the 30th September 1771 and so Kuhff and Fitzwater, prestigious confectioners with a business in the Haymarket in London, who were suppliers of confectionery to the Royal family, were invited to submit proposals to supply the refreshments.[26] These were quickly accepted by the committee and The Chronicle reported on the 19th. September that the two confectioners were already in Bath to prepare the sideboards. In anticipation the committee had already purchased from Messrs Cameron & Hogg 7lbs of isinglass and 7 lbs of hartshorn shavings, the traditional agents for setting jellies, that Kuhff and Fitzwater would have used in their preparations. They provided the ornaments for the front table, the sideboards and the beaufetts [buffets]. These, together with the glasses and the utensils they provided, were to be returned after the event. On the night of the Ridotto the doors of the Assembly Rooms opened at seven, the sideboards at nine, the confectionery tables were loaded with cakes, jellies, fruits and other delights and the ball ended at midnight. Kuhff and Fitzwater's bill was for £52 (£4,600 in modern values) with an extra 10 shillings 'for the teaspoons' and another 10 shillings for their servants' work at the opening the Ridotto.

Richard Brinsley Sheridan anonymously published[27] a satirical poem about the Ridotto written as a letter from a fictional waiter at the Rooms called Timothy Screw, employed by Kuhff and Fitzwater, to his brother, a waiter in a London Assembly Rooms. Here are a few of the verses that describe the supper at the Ball.

31st December 1789. Yale University Archives, ACC:98.8.16 (44.560). Thanks to Tatjana LeBoff for the reference.

26   Proceedings of the Committee for Managing the New Assembly Rooms in Bath 1771-1775: Typescript: p. 13, 17/9/1771, p.31, 27/10/1771. Bath Record Office: 0028A/5 & *Bath Chronicle*, 19/9/1771, pp. 1c &. 3d; 26/9/1771, p.1c.

27   *Bath Chronicle*, 2/1/1772, p. 1.c.

The Ridotto of Bath

A Panegyrick

Being an original epistle from Timothy Screw, Under-server to Messrs

K-hff and F –zw-ter, to his brother Henry, Waiter at Almack's

But, silence ye hautboys! Ye fiddles be dumb:

Ye dances stop instant – The HOUR is come;

The great! The all-wonderful hour – of EATING!

The hour, - for which ye all know you've been waiting:

Well the doors were unbolted, and in they all rushed:

They crowded, they jostled, they jockey'd and push'd;

In files they march'd up to the sideboards, while each

Laid claim upon all the good things in his reach;

There stuck to his part, cramm'd while he was able,

And then carried off all he could from the table;

Our outworks they storm'd with prowess most manful;

And jellies and cakes carried off by the handful;

While some our lines enter'd, with courage undaunted;

Nor quitted the trench 'till they'd got what they wanted.

However the viands went at such a rate,

A lady's toupee knock'd down a plate,

And many confess'd a fat citizen's belly;

A terrible stop to the progress of jelly;

While salvers of biscuits around their ears flew,

O'erturn'd by the whisk of an officer's queue*;

And thus in ten minutes one half of the treat,

Made a pretty check carpet squash'd under their feet:

[*the pony tail of a gentleman's wig]

Concerts were another entertainment available at the Assembly Rooms. Those in the Upper Rooms were led by the well-established Bath musician Thomas Linley and those in the Lower Rooms were led by Franz LaMotte, who had been brought to the Lower Rooms in October 1777 to compete with Linley. As a child musical prodigy LaMotte had played throughout Europe before coming Bath. The Franks paid the subscription to LaMotte's subscription concerts at the Lower Rooms when they first arrived in the city and on Wednesdays, 19th November and 3rd December, they went to Linley's concerts at the New Rooms. There were three of them in the party on the 19th, including Jacob's niece Abby [Abigail] Franks, the tickets were 5/- each and together with the cost of tea the total bill was 16/6d. Although there was competition between the concerts in the two sets of Rooms the same musicians performed in both. At Linley's concert Thomas Linley played the violin, his two daughters the Misses Linley, and Franz LaMotte provided the vocals together with Venanzio Rauzzini who was a new talent brought to Bath by LaMotte for his concerts at the Lower Rooms; Rauzzini would later become the dominant musical figure in Bath. Edward Rack describes attending a concert by LaMotte two years later in 1779 that took place in the Upper Assembly Rooms.

> Had a ticket sent me for the concert this evening at the New Rooms. After reflecting on the matter cooly, went thither and found the most brilliant assembly my eyes ever beheld. The elegance of the room illuminated with 480 wax candles, the prismatic colours of the lustres, the blaze of jewels, & the inconceivable harmony of near 40 musicians, some of whom are the finest hands in Europe, added to the rich attire of about 800 gentlemen and ladies was altogether a scene of which no person who never saw it can form any adequate idea. It began at half past 6 and ended at 10. The highest decorum was observ'd throughout the whole. The concertos by La Motte & Fischer surpass all description. Of the violin & oboe they are not equalid by any performer in Europe. They are both Italians –Rauzina [Rauzzini] is a eunich [eunuch]& has a fine shrill pipe. Near 60 of the nobility were present and several foreigners of distinction.[28]

Another musical figure in Bath was Michael Arne the son of Thomas Arne the composer of 'Rule Britannia' and the cash book records the purchase of tickets for a concert on the 29th November at the Lower Rooms when Arne played a harpsichord concerto. He and his wife had recently arrived from Dublin where she had become a very popular singer, and her performance at the concert was advertised as her first professional appearance in Britain.

On several Saturday evenings there is a terse entry - 'Play 4/-', at first glance these suggest that the Franks went to see plays at the Theatre Royal in Orchard Street on Saturdays. But in the eighteenth century the word 'play' could also mean gambling; showing how the cash book is sometimes elusive in its meaning. The alternate readings of these entries lead to very different lights

28   Journal of Edmund Rack, op cit. 29 December 1779, typescript p. 5, Bath Record Office.

on the Franks' reasons for visiting the city – cultural pleasures or gambling thrills. Judging which interpretation is most likely requires a look at the context.

The cash book only twice, and during much later visits to Bath, names the play seen, once in 1803 and once in 1807. On the first of these occasions on the 21st April 1803 (see frontispiece) the Franks bought three tickets for the play 'Pizarro' by Richard Sheridan, and then two days later bought '2 tickets for play tonight and three tickets for Thursday'. The tickets cost 4/- per person which was the cost of a box seat in the theatre. In these instances the term 'play' clearly refers to the theatre. Later entries on the 24th March refer to 'Play 9/-' and then 'ditto for servants – 10/6d'. These prices do not fit with the 4/- cost of a place in a box and so probably refer to seats in the pit which although no longer the raucous place it had been in the past was still only suitable for tradespeople and servants. Again the term play clearly meant dramas as it was unlikely that a master was paying his servants to gamble.

The contextual evidence for 'play' to mean not theatre but gambling comes from the common use of the term in that manner. William Brereton the Master of Ceremonies of the Lower Rooms in 1780 for example, as he was put in gaol for gambling debts, wrote 'PLAY is my passion –That PLAY is my support' though admitting that it had brought him low.[29] Gambling was such a feature of fashionable

The Theatre Royal in Orchard Street: courtesy of Akeman Press

Bath life that it seems likely that the Franks would have indulged, and in later years they had their own private card parties. In 1771 the price of a pack of cards in the Upper Rooms had been set at 6/- for two packs and 2/6d for each subsequent pack if two gentlemen were playing.[30] The four shillings noted in the cash book for 'play' would seem insufficient pay for the cards if the Franks were playing cards most Saturdays in the Rooms, but if they were playing at private parties four shillings may have covered the tips given to the footmen

29   Brereton, William, To the Ladies, Noblemen and Gentlemen subscribers to the Lower Rooms, 27/3/1780, Bath Record Office, Broadsides & Posters, no.83.

30   Proceedings of the Committee for Managing the New Assembly Rooms in Bath 1771-1775: manuscript & Typescript: Bath Record Office, ref: 0028A/6.

who had the perk of supplying the packs of cards.[31] However there is no clear evidence in the cash book until 1803 that the Franks gambled, and unless they are disguised under some obscure entry in the book or recorded in other account books there are no gambling gains or losses entered during this early visit. The tentative conclusion is that 'play' mostly refers to theatre visits.

So if rather than gambling the Franks were going to the theatre they would have seen each evening a main play followed by a shorter piece normally a farce, pantomime or comic opera. On their first Saturday they saw 'The Provok'd Wife' by John Vanbrugh. The short piece on this occasion was 'The Waterman'. Three weeks later on the 29th November one of the Franks went to 'The Way to Keep Him' by Arthur Murphy followed by the ever popular comic opera 'The Quaker'. It seems whoever went enjoyed the main play so much that the other two went to see it on the 13th December. On the subsequent three Saturdays the play-going Franks saw 'The Runaway' by Hannah Cowley; a new play that had been first performed in 1776; then 'The Jealous Wife' by George Colman together with a pantomime 'Bladud ' that told the story of the mythical foundation of Bath, and finally they were at John Dryden's 'The Spanish Fryer', with another performance of 'The Quaker'. It seems that the Franks missed the recent London theatrical success, Richard Brinsley Sheridan's 'School for Scandal', that had several performances in the Theatre Royal whilst they were in Bath.

If the entries for 'play' in the cash book had referred to gambling at cards a very different scene would have been conjured. Bath was notorious for high stakes gambling and wagering. The later evidence in the cash book of the Franks' card playing habits suggests that they played in private parties and for relatively low stakes.

GAMBLING AND CARD PLAYING IN BATH

Edmund Rack, a Quaker frequently commented on the amount of high stakes gambling that took place in the city, particularly in the Assembly Rooms. On the 22nd January in 1780 he wrote:[32] 'At 2 o'clock went to Rooms – 11 card tables – deep play – gold & bank notes very plentiful – what a stupid amusement!' Later that month

31   Fisher, C. (2016) *The A-Z of the Royal Crescent: Polite & Impolite Life in Eighteenth Century Bath*, ELSP, pp.76-77.

32   Rack, Edmund op cit.

he gave vent to his frustration at the waste caused by gambling.

> Stept into the New Rooms as I return'd. 17 card tables full – gold
> & notes to a considerable amount on each. What a pity when it is
> so much wanted. What insignificant beings! How did I wish at that
> moment for the Gorgon's snaky head to turn them all into stone
> and convert their treasure to a more rational use. Among all the
> municipal laws of this kingdom & publick hospitals, I wonder that the
> general interest of the people has not suggested the idea of building
> an hospital for gamesters and making a law that every person who
> shuffles cards and rattles dice for more than one shilling a game or
> throw shall forfeit his property to the State & be confin'd in said
> hospital as a lunatic till he has so far recovered his senses as to
> give bond for the forfeiture of half his property on conviction of a
> second offence.

Gambling wasn't restricted to card playing, In March he noted,
'After dinner went to Rooms – walked into the billiard room – high
betting between Sir Jno Lindsey & Sir Edwd Littleton, Col Horne
and Major Mallock'. There were also card sharper gangs, mostly
military officers, in the city known as the Greeks who were skilled
at grooming and fleecing unwary visitors to Bath. The *Morning Post*
reported in 1791:[33]

> Gaming rises hourly amongst us... A Mr O--- who some time ago
> made a successful trip to India no sooner showed his nose here
> than our knowing ones were down upon him... he made a wise
> match at billiards with the celebrated Mr P and put off 4,000 guineas
> before breakfast... Of all the pigeons an oriental one is found most
> palatable to our Bath gentry.

There were other pastimes available in Bath. There are several cash book
entries for playing billiards, a new billiard table had been installed in the Upper
Rooms in May 1775;[34] was Jacob playing, (were wagers involved) or did women

33 *Morning Post*, 24/1/1791 & 19/11/1791.

34 Minutes of the Committee for the Management of the New Rooms , 7/5/1775,
    Bath Record Office.

play billiards in the eighteenth century and it was Priscilla at the billiard table?
On the 25th November someone in the Franks party played tennis; this was
Real Tennis played at an indoor court that included a slope like a shed roof
along one side of the court that the ball could be bounced off. It was the
precursor of Lawn Tennis and there was a real tennis court at the end of Russell
Street near the Upper Assembly Rooms in a building that is now the Museum
of Bath at Work. The gunsmith was paid 7/6d and Jacob went shooting on the
15th November. For quieter moments the Franks joined a subscription library
of which there were several in the city. They probably joined the nearest to
them which was Andrew Tennent's at the corner of Milson Street that became
Bally & Clinch's circulating library in 1780.

The Real Tennis Court in Bath, now the Museum of Bath at Work: author's collection

Walking or riding to take the air in the city or the surrounding country
side was a familiar diversion (the Franks stabled their horses at York House
whose stable yard backed onto Milsom Street). They shopped in the toyshops
that sold fancy goods for grown-ups. For instance they ordered a seal to be
engraved at Wicksteed's, a process that had for many years been done at
'Wicksteed's machine' (a water powered gem engraving device); a favourite
tourist spot on Mr Allen's road in Widcombe. By 1777 Wicksteed's machine
had relocated to Pulteney Bridge.[35]

35   Brett, Vanessa (2014) *Bertrand's Toyshop in Bath: Luxury Retailing 1685-1765*, p.

The common way of getting about the city was to hire a chair, an enclosed chair carried on poles by two chairmen.[36] There were two types in use, the bath or bathing chair for transporting people between their bedrooms and the baths and the Sedan or the 'sedan glass' chair for visiting, going to the Assembly Rooms or the theatre. The original bathing chairs were carried between short poles to enable them to be taken into houses and were covered with cloth supported on hoops that went over and around the occupant's head, with a curtain at the front to protect privacy; they did not however protect from the rain. The Sedan chair was a larger stronger chair constructed in wood and leather and carried on long poles. They had glass windows and a door at the front to allow the customer in and out. From the 1740s there was a compromise between the two types of chair known as the close chair. It was used to take people bathing and so was smaller than a Sedan chair and used short poles. It had a wooden frame covered with stiff linen painted black and it bellied out at the bottom in the front to allow space for the occupant's feet. It was a little more comfortable and dignified than the old bathing chairs. Chairmen would often use close chairs in the morning which is when people went to bathe and Sedan chairs for the rest of the day; the Franks would have used both.

Often the Franks hired a Sedan chair and went out to a public breakfast or for tea. There are frequent entries for 'chair & tea', often taken in the New Rooms where the waiters would have been ever courteous in anticipation of tips. Occasionally tea did not quite hit the spot and they drank negus, a mulled wine - wine, water, sugar and nutmeg. On another occasion they bought diavolinos, which were sugar balls flavoured with either chocolate or peppermint.

CHAIRS AND CHAIRMEN

Chairs were the most convenient way for Bath society to move about the city and they were used frequently by the Franks; but the chairmen who carried them often terrified their customers. They seemed forbidding as they clustered around the doors of the Assembly Rooms and the theatre waiting for custom and every

183. Fawcett, T. (2009) *Bath Commercialis'd* , p.91.

36   Fawcett, Trevor, (1998) 'Chair Transport in Bath: the Sedan Chair', *Bath History*, Vol. II, pp. 113-138. The *Bath Chronicle* advertised 'two sedan glass chairs and two bathing chairs' for sale on 1/6/1775, p.3d.

chairman it was claimed had too many dogs, at least a terrier and a spaniel, and some had three or four of each kind, snapping around their, and their fare's, heels. A report in the Times in 1791 noted

'Being accelerated in one's progress by the lively application of a chairman's pole a posteriori': author's collection

another issue:

> The ladies were delayed some time on Monday evening in retiring from the Dress Ball at the New Rooms, on account of a fracas which happened among the Chairmen that was continued for some time in a very savage manner. Is a Lady of Honour sufficiently safe in the hands of two such brutes as generally carry chairs?[37]

Many visited Bath for their health and to take the waters; and even if one was in good health it seems it was obligatory to consult a doctor on arrival in the city. The Franks consulted Dr Philip De La Cour, the Sephardic Jewish doctor with practices in London and Bath. He visited the Franks several times for a fee of a guinea per visit, two of them were for consultations with 'Mrs F'. However there are no entries in the cash book during this first visit to the city for the fees that had to be paid to the 'pumpers' when people drank the mineral waters in the Pump Room, unless these were covered in a large final 'sundries' item of £49-4s.. There is however one payment of 1/- on the 12th November for 'Bath'. The charges for bathing at the Kings Bath (the new Hot Bath and the Kingston Baths were still being built in 1777) was 1/- although the Guide

---

37   *The Times*, 28/11/1791, p.3.

and the Cloth Woman who obtained the bathing linen[38] also had to be paid a small fee.

So it is probable that someone in the Franks' party went once to bathe in the hot mineral waters but it was clearly not a major part of their visit to Bath, nor was it always advisable. Philip Thicknesse pointed out that bathing in the hot waters could be medically counter-productive if the patients were not really ill; 'and it is to be suspected that many who had supposedly come to Bath for their health had actually come for the society and its amusements'. Even if actually ill, before bathing 'Evacuations are absolutely necessary to unload the habit, and clean out the first passages, among which Vomits are often necessary, safe and useful'. He also recommended that, when bathing, the head should only be immersed when the patient was about to leave the baths.

Tips and charitable giving were a key aspect of a visit to Bath, especially as the Franks were there in the Christmas season. On the 23rd December they sent a 'Xmas box' of 15/6d to the Lower Rooms and on Christmas Day a 10/6d 'Xmas box' to Mr Dawson's [Upper] Rooms and when leaving Bath the Franks gave the Porter at the Upper Rooms a tip of 5/-d. Even if someone was invited to dinner at a private house they would be expected to tip all the household servants when they left. The Franks also went to a charity sermon on the 14th December and contributed 1/-d.

Tip giving and what is now known as 'grease' or facilitation payments may explain a curiosity in the Franks' cash book. There are nine entries mentioning 'gloves' in an eight week period. Was this more than can be accounted for by buying pairs of gloves? Gloves was also an eighteenth century slang term for a present or a bribe[39] and 'gloves' is often listed in the cash book in connection with an excursion - hiring a sedan chair, going to a ball or play, going shopping for perfumery or for a glass of negus - so it is probable that gloves were a tip or 'grease' that had to be paid to get a service?

At the end of December the visit to Bath was coming to an end and the Franks settled all their bills including those for the house rent, horse keeping at York House and rental of a harpsichord. The tradesmen's bills to paid included Dodd the apothecary (£5-18s-9p), Henry Derham the wine merchant[40] (£5-

38   The prices are quoted in Thicknesse, op cit. p .47.

39   *Oxford English Dictionary*: glove money – a gratuity given to servants ostensibly to buy them gloves; Francis Grosse (1785) *The Vulgar Tongue*: to make a present or bribe.

40   Derham was a wine merchant to the New Rooms and by 1788 Derham & Stroud's wine vaults were located at the New Rooms, *Bath Chronicle* 2/5/1788.

1s-8d), the brewer Bywater (£4-8s), Williams the woollen draper, Webb the grocer, the hairdresser (£2-15s) and among the household staff the housemaid received 2s-2d. Philip Thicknesse:

> advised against leaving settling bills until the day visitors left the city when they do not have time to examine their Bills with Attention, nor to see they are fairly cast up by which means, they are often grossly imposed upon, and if they do not take the receipt stand a Chance of finding a Duplicate, of that Bill when they return another season, or at the top of a *fresh* Bill --- *Left unpaid last year.*'[41]

The Franks closed the account on the 2nd January 1778 and the total cost of the visit to Bath was £377-12s-9d [£32,500 in 2017 spending power]. They headed home to Isleworth taking the Bath Road to London and turning right at the turnpike near Sion House from where it was just a few miles to Twickenham, Hampton Court and Isleworth.

By 1791 Derham and Stroud were reported to be co-managers of the Rooms.

41   Thicknesse op cit. p.64.

4
A BRITISH GRAND TOUR: 1778:
THE EXCURSIONS THROUGH THE MIDLANDS AND THE NORTH

IN SUMMER 1778 the Franks decided to make a grand tour of the north of England that was to take in spas, (with their health giving wells and opportunities for balls), stately homes, the seaside, horse race meetings and, given that the north was rapidly industrialising, visits to factories and industrial sites. There would also be shopping.

The Franks left Isleworth on the 21st July 1778 and arrived at Oxford on the 22nd. They lodged at the Star, bought a 'book of directions' and took a tour of the University that cost 14/-. They then took a chaise to the Oxford Races that were held from the 21st to the 23rd. At the races, according to the newspaper announcement,[42] ordinaries would be available as usual; they were set price meals consisting of a hot dish, bread and ale that could be had at the inns near the race course. There were also ladies' ordinaries available, as well as a public breakfast each morning of the race meet. Jacob and Priscila attended one of the balls at the Town Hall that were held during the races and they even managed to fit in a concert. Whilst they were busy enjoying Oxford they had their carriage washed and greased.

As they left Oxford they visited Blenheim Palace at Woodstock and tipped the housekeeper half a guinea and the porter half a crown. Blenheim was a must see tourist stop that had been designed by Sir John Vanbrugh and Nicholas Hawksmoor as a palace to reward John Churchill, 1st Duke of Marlborough for his famous victory at Blenheim in the War of Spanish Succession.

From Oxford the Franks travelled to 'Daintree' [Daventry] where they gave a shilling to the boys at the wig makers and then passed through

Lutterworth to nearby Misterton Hall[43] which was the country house of Jacob's uncle Naphtali (Heartsey) Franks. They gave a tip to the bell ringers of Lutterworth; perhaps a peal of bells had announced their arrival at Misterton? Aaron Franks, Priscilla's father, acting as his father's executor had bought the estate in 1753 to fulfil his father's wishes to provide for his grandchildren; and the estate passed to Naphtali. When Naphtali died in 1796 Jacob Henry Franks, one of the grandchildren, inherited Misterton Hall and became Lord of the Manor. Naphtali was an enthusiastic gardener and had brought pines over from America to plant in the Hall's parkland. Jacob Henry's son became the vicar of Misterton.

Misterton Hall, Leicestershire: permission of Leicestershire Record Office.

Coventry was the next stop where they admired the churches and visited the manufactory. Coventry at that time was famous for producing silk ribbons. It was a long established female homeworking industry that in the early 1800s employed half of the city's population. It was an industry that would soon be in decline, because of a switch to production by machines in factories and by cheap imports. In 1861 the ladies of Bath organised a Coventry Ribbon Ball in the Assembly Rooms to raise money for the destitute women weavers of Coventry. By 1778 in contrast the watch making cottage industry in the city had already made great productivity improvements through new techniques, increased specialisation and division of labour so that the average price of a silver watch fell from £6 in 1710 to £2 in 1810; and cheaper watches could be had for about 4s.[44] There is

Matthew Boulton's Soho Manufactory in Birmingham: Look & Learn Historical Picture Archive

43   Brown, Malcolm (1981-2) 'Anglo-Jewish Country houses from the Resettlement to 1800', Transactions and Miscellanies, (Jewish History Society of England) Vol. 28, p26.

44   Kelly, M. & O'Grada, K. (2016) 'Adam Smith, Watch prices and the Industrial

a cryptic entry in the cash book – 'watch Belle 4s' suggesting that the Franks took advantage of this manufacturing productivity. The identity of Belle is uncertain but a possible recipient of the watch was Isabella Bell Franks, Jacob and Priscilla's ten year old great niece.

Birmingham was the Franks' next stop where again the point of interest was new developments in manufacturing. They visited the factory of Matthew Boulton [spelt Bolton in the cash book] at Soho that had been completed in 1766. Matthew Boulton was a toy manufacturer and in Georgian times toys were not for children but fancy goods for adults. He specialised in silver buttons and buckles, japanned ware and ormolu, gilded bronze. Boulton was a member of the Lunar Society which met at his home Soho House and whose members included Erasmus Darwin, Josiah Wedgwood and Joseph Priestley the chemist. The Franks paid 7/6d to tour the works and bought a comb, a toothpick, a snuff box 'for DS' and 'pamboxes for the ladies'. These are a mystery but Pam was a popular card game also known as Five Card Loo and so the boxes were probably japanned ware card boxes. They also gave 2/6d to a sick boy at the Works.

Whilst in Birmingham their carriage may have needed repair because there was a coach maker's bill for £2-12-8d. The Franks also bought a copy of *Tristram Shandy* the novel by Laurence Sterne; its episodic, shaggy dog story nature probably made it a good read for long coach journeys. After Birmingham the tour continued north east to Nottingham which, as it was famed for its framework knitters and hosiery, they bought stockings; and then onto Sheffield, a metal working city. There they bought spurs, scissors, a pair of candelabra branches, a pair of 'sealing sticks', a pair of snuffers, a watch chain, canes and a pair of bracelets 'for AF', Abigail Franks, Jacob's niece and Jacob Henry's sister, who had been to Bath with Jacob and Priscilla the year before.

Most of August 1778 was spent at Harrogate, a well-known spa town and at nearby Knaresborough. On their arrival both Jacob and Priscilla consulted Dr Kilvington a local physician. The town had both an iron-rich chalybeate spring and a sulphurous one. No doubt the Franks took the waters at both of them and compared their effects with those of Bath mineral water. They also paid a visit to Knaresborough and an entry in the book for half a crown for 'the maid at the well' suggests they visited Mother Shipton's Well, said to be the earliest entrance-charging tourist attraction in England, having opened in 1630. It was a petrifying well that caused anything placed in it to became hardened to stone. A few days later the Franks visited Harewood House (5/6d to the house keeper), designed by John Carr the architect and

The Chalybeate well at Harrogate, 1796, by John Raphael Smith: courtesy of the Royal Academy of Arts

Robert Adam who was responsible for the interior decoration, which was still being completed in 1778. The house was built for Edwin Lascelles who had made his fortune as a director of the East India Company and was the owner of a West Indian sugar plantation. Whilst they were in the area they paid a visit to 'Mr D. Lascelles Plumpton'. This was Daniel Lascelles (1714-1784), Edwin Lascelles' brother, who was also a West Indian plantation owner and a Member of Parliament; Plompton Hall[45] (as it is now spelt) located between Harrogate and Knaresborough was one of his properties. Lascelles' main seat, not far distant from Plompton, was Goldsborough Hall that he moved into in 1762. Like Harewood it had been designed by John Carr. The Franks family also were part owners of a sugar plantation and perhaps Jacob and Lascelles discussed West Indian affairs.

Jacob Franks went shooting whilst in Harrogate. He bought a pointer dog on the 5th August and a dog collar and chain a few days later and on the 19th he was a member of a shooting party with Dr Kilvington. Towards the end of the month the Franks spent four days at the York Races. There is one

45   Historic England (n.d) Plompton Hall and Flanking Walls, historicengland.org. uk.

of the cryptic entries in the cash book during their time at the races, 'paid Firemen at York for a pair of gloves – 2/3'. Treating it as a cryptic clue, the *Oxford English Dictionary* gives an old definition of fireman as a zealous and fervent man, and as we have seen, gloves could refer to a bribe, so was Jacob Franks paying off a difficult person or was he just buying a pair of gloves from a glover named Fireman?

Mother Shipton's Well at Knaresborough, Engraving c 1771 from an earlier engraving of 1746-7, by Francis Vivares after Thomas Smith: Yale Center for British Art, Paul Mellon Collection

After York the next destination for the Franks was Scarborough and on the way there they visited another Vanbrugh and Hawksmoor house, Castle Howard, for a fee of 5/- to the housekeeper. The journey from Harrogate to Scarborough, which was another popular spa town, cost £12-4-6d. Richard Brinsley Sheridan's comic play 'A trip to Scarborough' had been performed at Drury Lane London the previous year attesting to the resort's fame. The play and the place inspired a caricature with the same title.

The Franks spent just over two weeks at Scarborough. The town's earliest Assembly Room, or Long Room as they were also known, was built right on the shoreline but by the time the Franks arrived it was no longer fashionable and there were two new well-appointed places for balls and entertainment, the Assembly Rooms and Donner's Rooms on St Nicholas Street, also known

A trip to Scarborough 1783 by James Brotherton: Look & Learn Historical Picture Archive

as Long Room Street, in the Upper Town. On their arrival the Franks paid the one guinea subscriptions to the Assembly Rooms and Donner's Rooms. During their stay they attended three balls including the Master of Ceremonies Benefit ball. Jacob seems to have done more shooting and taken several sailing trips. There were payments for dinners and suppers, 5/6 was spent on a raffle and the couple saw a play.

Whilst they were in Scarborough they seem to have taken lodgings from a Mr Glass and then paid for a local cook and housemaid, who probably came with the lodgings, to support their own servants who had travelled with them. Amongst the latter was Clarke, who was with them in Bath the previous winter and who was occasionally paid for washing, 'house' and sundries during the tour and William for whom a pair of boots was bought at York.

When it was time to leave Scarborough the cash book mentions settling the bills of the butcher, the grocer, the cook and housemaid (2 guineas) and the shoe cleaner. Horses were an expensive item, post chaise horses for two weeks cost £6, ostler & grazing, 10/6d, shooting horses (for shooting parties) 17/6d and three horses for hackney [carriages]were 8/6d. The waiters at the Assembly Rooms and Donner's Rooms were each tipped 5/-d.

Jacob and Priscilla left Scarborough on the 17th September and travelled to Buxton, another spa town where they spent a couple of days before moving onto Manchester where they visited the Duke of Bridgewater's canal and coal pits. The Duke owned underground coal mines at Worsley and the canal was opened in 1761 to transport the coal to Manchester. It was the first canal to be dug in England and as the mines were up in the hills a series of underground canals and inclined planes had been constructed to bring the coal from the coal face to the surface canal for onward transportation to Manchester; where Jacob and Priscilla explored the town and the works. They arrived back at Isleworth on the 27th September.

5
COFFEE HOUSES AND SHOPPING:
BATH, WINTER SEASON, 1784

THE NEXT ENTRY in the cash book recording a visit to Bath is seven years later at Christmas 1784. The party consisted Jacob, Priscilla, Jacob's father David and Abby Franks, Jacob's niece. She is known to have been in the party because at the end of the trip Jacob paid for 'Abby's maid' to return to London by the stage coach.

Jacob and Priscilla may have made an earlier visit to the city in November 1779, the *Bath Chronicle* and the *Bath Journal*[46] reported the arrival of a Mr & Mrs Franks but if this was Jacob and Priscilla the trip was not recorded in the cash book. David Franks, Jacob's father, had been in the city in 1782 having removed himself from New York. As a loyalist during the American War of Independence (1775-1783) David Franks had been hounded by the American radicals in Philadelphia and had moved to New York and then to London where he arrived on the 2nd July 1782.[47] He had not been able to bring much of his money with him and applied to the British government for a loyalist pension which took some time to be approved, so he lived with Jacob and Priscilla at Isleworth and accompanied them on their visits to Bath. In September 1782 David wrote to colleagues in America whilst preparing to travel to Bath; the 'arrivals' sections of the Bath newspapers in January and February 1783 record only the arrival of a single Mr Franks so it is likely that Jacob and Priscilla did not accompany David on this occasion.

Jacob and Priscilla's 1777 visit set the pattern for this one with the exception that they stayed in lodgings at Mr J. Salmon's at £4-5s per week rather than renting a house. The 1791 *Bath Directory* lists two entries for a Mr J. Salmons who owned lodging houses, one at No.2 Bladud Buildings and one at No. 4 Oxford Row, the two houses are not far apart and the Franks could

46   *Bath Chronicle*, 18/11/1779, p.3b, *Bath Journal*, 15/11/1779, p.4d.

47   Stern op cit, p.163.

have been staying in either. They set about making themselves comfortable by buying the things their lodgings lacked – an extra pair of candlesticks, a mustard pot, a corkscrew, a brush and soap. They engaged the services of the cook and the maid who looked after the lodgings and ordered coal from Mr J. Croome the coal merchant in New King Street.[48]

Soon after they arrived on the 17th December the Franks paid the subscriptions for Balls at the Lower Rooms (1 guinea) and 10/- for the 'walking 'subscription; particularly useful on wet days when exercise could be taken in the comfort of the ball room. Then at the Upper Rooms they subscribed to the Dress Ball, three Cotillion Balls and 'walking for ladies'. Two days later they also paid for the Cotillion Balls at the Lower Rooms. By the time they had paid the library subscription they were set up for their stay in the city.

Mr Richard Tyson the Master of the Ceremonies of the Lower Rooms: courtesy of Michael Birkett-Jones.

The Franks attended the benefit balls for the Masters of Ceremonies, for Mr Tyson, the new Master of the Ceremonies at the Lower Rooms, on the 6th January and for Mr Dawson at the Upper Rooms on the 2nd January. Both were well attended by the 'nobility and gentry', nearly 900 at the Lower Rooms and 1,100 at the Upper Rooms.[49] The Franks by attending the benefit balls were paying homage to the Kings of Bath (as the Masters of the Ceremonies were often called). No doubt they felt obliged to do so because otherwise the Masters of the Ceremonies would have sought them out when they first arrived in Bath and paid them a visit. This is what happened in 1790 to Philip Francis who had been a member of the Supreme Council of Bengal and was a Member of Parliament. When he was in Bath; he wrote 'All the masters of

---

48   The details of the tradesmen the Franks dealt with during this stay are taken from the *Bath Directory* of 1791, indexed in the Bath Ancestors database, and Fawcett.(2009) *Bath Commercialis'd* op cit.

49   *Bath Chronicle*, 6/1/1785, p. 3d.

ceremonies in the world have been waiting upon me but if they wait 'till I wait on them they will have a pretty waiting job of it'.[50] Tyson was a stickler for the privileges of rank. In Richard Warner's satire 'Rebellion in Bath'[51] the 'Signora Rattana (a parody of Miss Wroughton[52]) says of him 'And solemn Mr T____, too, the stiff and tall, by nature form'd director of the ball, who skill'd in rank, deep vers'd in etiquette, e'er named me for the final minuet'. Notwithstanding the Franks' relative lack of rank they were of sufficient station to contribute the cost of their tickets to the Masters of Ceremonies' benefits.

If the Franks' social status was weakened by their social origins, being Jewish in their case, so was Richard Tyson's social provenance questioned. There were rumours that he was from a colonial family, the sugar plantation owning Tysons of St Kitts in the West Indies. Such families may have been wealthy but were regarded with social disdain. The gossip even considered that Tyson was mixed race, with a British father and an African mother. A letter to '*The Times*' in 1785 commenting on a dispute that had happened in the Assembly Rooms said of Tyson that; 'though a creole and not very fair'. (Was this a play on words; fair as both just and of a pale complexion?) This comment may just have been a casual slur but Tyson did have connections to St Kitts, in his will he mentioned an investment in the Conarees sugar plantation on the island.[53] Gossip about degrees of social station and people's places within them was the stuff of Bath social life.

50   Letter from Philip Francis, a postscript dated 1st January 1790 to a letter dated 31s December 1789, Yale University Archives, ACC:98.8.16 (44.560). Thanks to Tatjana LeBoff for the reference.

51   'Peter Paul Pallet' (Richard Warner), (1808) *Rebellion in Bath, or the Battle of the Upper Rooms*, London, p.28.

52   The satirical portraits in the 'Rebellion in Bath' and in Warner's 'Bath Characters' are identified in a letter by W. Siddons to Mrs Piozzi dated 24/12/1807. Burnim, Kalman A. (1969) The Letters of Sarah and William Siddons to Hester Lynch Piozzi in the John Rylands Library, p.87. Available online at: https://www.escholar.manchester.ac.uk/api/datastream?publicationPid=uk-ac-man-scw:1m2929&datastreamId=POST-PEER-REVIEW-PUBLISHERS-DOCUMENT.PDF. Miss Wroughton was a well-known socialite and often said to be one of the Queens of Bath, White, B (2011) 'But who was the Queen of Bath?' *Bath History*, Vol. XII, 43-61.

53   *The Times* 15/10/1785 p.3c; There is another possible, but not certain, reference to Tyson as a 'mulatto' in a Letter from Amabel Lucas to her sister Mary, Baroness Grantham, undated but reckoned summer 1775; Bedfordshire Archives and Record Service, Wrest Park (Lucas) Mss, L30/13/12/30. See also: Maria Grace (2020) 'Black Communities in Jane Austen's England', Jane Austen Variations, Blog:https://austenvariations.com/black-communities-in-jane-austens-england/. Will of Richard Tyson, National Archives PROB 11/1640/100, probate 1/2/1821.

The Franks also paid 10/6d for three tickets for the Birthday Ball at the Lower Rooms on the 18th January 1785 to celebrate the birthday of Queen Charlotte; it was 'brilliant and crowded' and the ticket price included 'tea, jellies, cakes, negus etc.', refreshments that normally were at extra charge at a ball. Throughout the day the city's churches rang their bells in celebration and the Mayor put on a cold collation at the Guildhall for the 'Corporation and their friends'.[54]

A NEW MASTER OF THE CEREMONIES

By the time of the Franks second visit to Bath in 1784 William Brereton was no longer Master of Ceremonies in the Lower Rooms. His departure was ignominious.[55] In April 1780 he resigned the position partly because he was deeply in debt and bound for debtor's prison (though he promised never to gamble again if he was allowed to retain his position[56]) but also because of the behaviour of his son-in-law George Brereton who was a renowned gambler, card cheat and duellist. George Brereton was in dispute with a Captain Spooner whom he had cheated out of a large sum of money at cards. This eventually led to a duel on Claverton Down at which Spooner was severely wounded. However the offence that broke the Assembly Room's rules was that Brereton paraded around the town, and in the Assembly Rooms, wearing his sword; and the Assembly Rooms committee concluded that William Brereton had not done everything in his power to prevent George displaying his sword in the 'public Rooms'. The subscribers to the Rooms were called upon to elect a new Master of Ceremonies. Alicia Macartney an independently wealthy woman of great social and political influence was much despised, and feared in the city (and called behind her back Mother Mac) supported the candidature of Richard Tyson. He was the Master of Ceremonies at Tunbridge Wells and had applied but failed to be appointed to the same role at Bath three years earlier when Mr Wade had resigned as Master of the

---

54   *Bath Chronicle*, 20/1/1785, p. 3d.

55   *Bath Chronicle*, 17/2/1780. p3, 6/4/1780, p. 1., 30/3/1780.

56   Brereton, William, To the Ladies, Noblemen and Gentlemen subscribers to the Lower Rooms, 27/3/1780, Bath Record office, ref. Broadsides & Posters, No. 83.

Ceremonies of both Rooms. The following extracts from a satirical verse lampooning Macartney's influence in the election are in the manner of Old Testament:

> And the strange woman [Macartney] lift up her voice and cried aloud ye children of the Lower Parts of the City, let this man, [Tyson] Yea my own be chosen, or I will root up the extremities of the Town, the backside of the Kingdom of Bladud shall be desolate, the Tabernacle [Assembly Rooms] shall tremble, & deadly shall be the Ruin. Thereof, Behold your King.
>
> So her Man was chosen, now the man came from a Strange Land*, and the Other Man who was thrust aside, was known unto the People.[57]
>
> But all this while William [Brereton] was in prison and his sickness was sore, but the people were all merciful unto Him, and said with one Voice, he is a Man of Sorrow and we will not forsake him in the Day of His Adversity.

(*Was this 'strange land' Tunbridge Wells or St Kitts?)

Alicia Macartney was proud of her involvement in the election. She wrote to a friend on the 20th May 1780:[58] 'The first of my plagues arose from Brereton being sent to jail which with his vices enforced the necessity of a new master of ceremonies... & unwilling to have any interference with the publick here – helped me in a state of neutrality – till I found that every trick was playing to exclude Mr Tyson the only proper one of them who had tho' a man of worth no other chance than my patronage – I espoused his cause so warmly that in nine days I got him elected by a majority of 136 – such a victory over their combinations was astonishing'.

A benefit ball was held to raise money for Mrs Brereton and by the end of March Brereton's household property was being auctioned to pay his creditors.

57   Henry Sandford, Commonplace book, manuscript, vol. 2, pp.101- 104. National Library of Ireland, Ms 9,844. Available on the World Wide Web, http://catalogue.nli.ie/Record/vtls000531018#page/1/mode/1up

58   Letter from A. Macartney 20/5/1780, Hertfordshire Archives and Local Studies, ref AH228.

The concerts the Franks attended were mostly the subscription series held at the Upper Rooms on Wednesdays; at the 5th January 1785 concert they treated themselves to tea. The performers at these concerts were not paid a fee but made their income from their benefit concerts. Jacob, Priscilla and David Franks attended the benefit for Mr Fischer, an acclaimed oboist, at the Upper Rooms, (the oboe was David Franks favourite instrument[59]) and then attended the benefit for the singer Marie Chanu that was held in the early afternoon. Mr Rauzzini's concerts were very popular, by this time he was the leading musician in Bath, and the Franks bought tickets on the 24th January for his benefit concert. Saturday evenings were still, probably, theatre night and they saw, again, 'The Jealous Wife', and for the first time 'The Chapter of Accidents' and 'The Pilgrim with entertainments'.

The Franks made a few changes in their habits during this second stay. There were many visits to Molland's the confectioners at No. 2 Milsom Street, one visit on the 20th December was after the only occasion one of them bathed in the hot mineral water baths. Molland's, one of the most expensive and fashionable confectioners in the city, alongside Gill's of Wade's Passage, specialised in savoury and sweet take-away food but they also had eating rooms on the premises.

MOLLAND'S: THE PASTRY COOKS

Jane Austen's heroine in the novel *'Persuasion'* famously visits Molland's the confectioners. Peter and Dorothea Molland were originally from Brighton but opened a shop in Northgate in Bath and then in 1782 opened the Milsom Street shop. They advertised 'all sorts of made dishes, soups and pastry, as neat and respectable as in London, dinners elegantly dressed, and especially at any set time sent to lodgings. Great variety of Biscuits. Dinners dressed at gentlemen's houses – Hot Pastry and Soup from twelve to four – French, Black and White Puddings – very Fine Turtle every day'.[60] The shop also features in a satirical verse titled 'The Wonders of a Week in Bath' published in 1811[61] as a popular resort of the fashionable young.

59   Stern, op cit, p. 166.

60   *Bath Chronicle*, 12/12/1784, p. 1d.

61   Anon (1811) *The Wonders of a Week in Bath: in a doggerel verse address to the Hon T.S____, from T____ Esq.*, p.10.

So, you know, t'would be foolish to sweat and pay,
To see the long legs of the girls at the play*,
You've the same sights for nothing each day,
T'is for this a crony of mine takes his stand,
At the door of the temple that's kept by Molland,
Immortal Molland! As immortal as Gill,
Were I like our Anstey on Helicon's Hill;
And thus with his eyes, and a couple of glasses,
He views all the charms of each nymph that passes;
Till at last all on fire at the sight of Miss S-----
He quenches his flame with a basin of soup.

*Women actors known as 'breeches actresses' would play male
parts in the theatre as an excuse to exhibit shapely legs in breeches.

Most of the Franks' meals would have been eaten at their lodging and prepared by the cook. They bought their groceries from George Shied of No. 34 Brock Street and their wine from Henry Derham as they had in their previous stay. By 1780s Derham's wine vaults were at Fountains Buildings near York House and he advertised Madeira wine at 27/- per dozen bottles, it could be delivered at 6/-a gallon with a deposit payable for the bottles that was redeemable when they were returned empty. Their beer came from Warren & Co brewers. This was James Warren Esq owner of the Walcot Porter Brewery that was located on the London Road near the Walcot Turnpike toll gates.[62] Three years earlier Warren, was so solicitous for the reputation of his porter that he had to advertise a warning against those who were selling inferior beer claiming it was from his brewery. Warren lived at Walcot House near St Michael's but died in 1789 in Nice where he had gone for his health.

Occasionally the Franks bought treats, nuts and peppers on one day, cream cheese on another and then oysters, although these were not then the delicacy that they are today. They also bought cheese to 'send to town'

62   Bath Ancestors: parish rates 1781: house and brewery belonging to James Warren in the 'outpart' of the parish. Adverts in the Chronicle 6/8/1789 & 26/11/1789 confirm the brewery was next to the turnpike. The turnpike tollgate was then at the junction with Snow Hill, later it was moved to Grosvenor at the junction with St Saviour's Road. The parish rate books records James Warren living on Walcot Street.

presumably to their house in London. However the Franks ate out more often during this stay. They dined at The Bear at the top of Stall Street, that Thicknesse thought the best inn after York House,[63] and at the White Hart opposite the Pump Room; there is also an entry of 2/- paid at Pickwick's on the 27th December, this was probably either Eleazer Pickwick who ran the White Hart as well as owning a lucrative carrier business or his nephew Moses Pickwick. There are also entries for attending a Public Breakfast.

There was more evidence of shopping on this visit. Jacob bought a 'sattin waistcoat' and two waistcoats for 'PB' as well as a boot jack, a pair of boot stretchers and a pair of black silk stockings. One named Bath tradesman who was patronised was William Basnett the goldsmith, jeweller and toyman, and a vendor of fossils, from whom a pair of shoe buckles and coat buttons were purchased. Until 1780 when he gave up that line of business Basnett was also a print seller and as can be seen from his advertisement his range of stock was wide.[64]

MR BASNETT'S STOCK-IN-TRADE

An advertisement in the *Bath Chronicle* on the 11th April 1771 itemises the merchandise.

Paste Buckles, Stay hooks, Ear-rings; Pins and Combs; Pearl, Coque and Marcasite Drop and Top Ear-rings; Venetian-pearl and Bead Collars and Ear-rings: Seals mounted in Gold, Silver & Pinchbeck; Enamell'd, plain and grav'd Gold Sleeve Buttons, Mocho and Crystal ditto in Gold and Silver, Gilt and Enamell'd ditto; Fancy and Hoop Rings, Wires, Locketts, Broaches, Trinkets etc Elegant Toilets in Tortoise-shell and Blue Fish-skin, Morocco Etwees, Gilded, Glass, Toilet and Essence Bottles; Enamell'd Candle- sticks mounted in Silver, Sets of castors in Silver Frames; Silver and Gilt Philagree Needle Books, Toothpicks and Bottle Cases, Silver Pencil and Pen Cases, Decanter Corks, silver and gilt Thimbles, plain and chased Eggs; neat Silver, Pinchbeck and Gilt Buckles, black & blue ditto, fine and steel and gilt Watch Chains, curious Scissars, Best London Penknives, neat

63   Thicknesse op cit, p.62. The Bear Inn stood at the bottom of what is now Union Street, which did not then exist so the only route down from Milsom Street to the Pump Room was Union Passage then known as Cock lane.

64   *Bath Chronicle* 23/3/1780, p. 3d. Basnett Receipt, Ephemera Collection, TCB/016/1, Bath Record Office.

Sheffield Pocket and Fruit Knives, Mahogany Cases with Razors, Steel Snuffers and Stands, Card Snuffers and Douters, Cork Screws, best London plated Bitts, Stirrups, Spurs, etc. Telescopes, Spectacles, Microscopes, Concaves, Opera, Prospect Diagonal and Reading Glasses, Mathematical Instruments; Bamboo, japan and other Walking Canes, Paper Snuff Boxes, Toothpicks, Bottle and Ink cases, Pearl Shuttles, Bottle Labels and Tea Tongs, neat Card and Work Bags, Fish Baskets and Thread Cases, rich velvet and Gold Etwees, Pincushions, Spotted and Plain Purses, Backgammon tables, Combs and Brushes, Toupee and Pinching Irons, Powder Knives, Purse and Tambour Needles, etc. etc.

The shop in 1784 was at No 1 Bond Street in a building that no longer exists located at the southern end of Milsom Street. It had a prominent position near the junctions with Quiet and Green Street and faced up Milsom Street. As such it blocked the route from the Upper to Lower towns allowing only a narrow passageway through to Union Passage, which was itself notoriously crowded. Consequently, under the provisions of the Bath Improvement Acts of 1789 and 1810 that led to the creation of New Bond Street and Union Street, the shop and house were demolished and Basnett moved his premises in 1810 to No. 28 Milsom Street.[65]

Jacob Franks paid £1-14s to Thomas Parsons who was the leading breeches maker in town. Ordinary cloth breeches were made by tailors but breeches makers like Parsons, who had his shop at No. 19 Northgate Street, made breeches from leather - buck, doe or sheep skin. They also made other leather goods such as gloves and satchels. Leather breeches were fashionable and had even been allowed in the Assembly Rooms until 1765 when they were banned as 'unsuited to the decorum of the place'. Jacob occasionally bought, something all Georgian gentlemen needed, a breeches ball which was a clay-like cake (main ingredient Bath Brick) used to cover stains and marks on breeches. If gloves were also being bought at Parsons the Franks were just in time because in 1785 a 20% tax was applied to a pair of gloves. Parsons continued trading at Northgate Street until 1801. The bills of Mr Wilson the tailor, probably the Thomas Wilson the 'man's mercer' of St Andrews Terrace, were the next to be paid.

Textiles were bought from Christopher Marsh the woollen draper of Abbey Yard and from Arthur Jones of Cheap Street, another woollen draper,

65   Hunt Collection, Vol. 3, p. 166, Bath Record Office; *Bath Chronicle*, 23/7/1789, p.1b, 13/9/1810, 7/11/1811.

Union Passage in 1801 crowded with sedan chairs, invalid 'gouty' chairs and pedestrians: permission of Bath Record Office

from whom they bought a bale of 'cassimere' [Kashmir or pashmina] often used for shawls. The cheaper Muslin textile they bought from a Mrs Cowling who also did their laundry. A 'pair of ruffles were bought', they were a frilled strip of lace or silk used as ornament for the wrist; as both men and women wore them we do not know if they were for Jacob, Priscilla or Abby. The services of the hairdresser Mr J Taylor of Trim Street were employed and 'his man' was tipped several times, but again we do not know whether it was Jacob, David, the women or all four using his talents.

BATH SHOPKEEPERS: PROSPERITY & ANXIETY

Bath was a good place to be a shopkeeper because it was full of visitors with money but there was fierce competition for trade. Between 1770 and 1780 the number of linen drapers in the city doubled from seven to fourteen. Even when the merchants were doing well there was always an anxiety that good times could come to an end. This was felt very strongly in 1780 when Bath and London experienced the anti-Catholic Gordon Riots. In Bath on the night of the 9th of June a mob rampaged in the city setting fire to the Catholic chapel, the presbytery and other buildings. This so alarmed Francis Bennett a prosperous retired draper who had owned a shop in Abbey churchyard that he wrote to the Mayor demanding that 'this almost ruined city' be put in a 'proper posture of defence before it is too late'. He thought that the mob was preparing to renew its destruction in the city and hinted that unless something was done that he and others who had invested in the city would have to leave. 'It is true I have spent many thousands in this city, and that with a deal of pleasure and satisfaction, and would be heartily sorry to leave it on account of a destructive and rebellious set of ruffians'.[66]

Something was done. John Butler, a footman at No. 6 Royal Crescent was hanged in public for his part in the riots[67] on the 28th August 1780. Executions were generally held at Taunton the county town of Somerset but on this occasion the hanging was in Bath as a warning to those in the city who might be contemplating civic violence. The gallows were set up near the junction of Westgate Buildings and St James's Parade not far from where the riot had happened. The cart bearing John Butler, accompanied by his brother, brother-in-law and a vicar, to the gallows was led by the city constables followed by the chairmen (who often acted as an auxiliary security force in the city) and the Javelin men [the High Sherriff's body guard] as a display to reinforce the city's intention to maintain its prosperous commerce.

66   Neale, R. S. (1981) *Bath, A Social History 1680-1850 or a Valley of Pleasure yet a Sink of Iniquity*, London: Routledge & Kegan Paul, p.p. 311-312.

67   Fisher, op cit, pp 185-186.

One item that would have been bought for Priscilla or Abby's beauty preparation was the 'court plaisters' purchased for 4d. These were strips of satin coated on one side with a mixture of isinglass and glucose; they were much used in the eighteenth century as beauty patches for the face; but by the 1780s they were going out of fashion and may have been used medicinally. The Franks did spend on everyday medicines such as 'eye water', rose water and lozenges. They bought many of their medicines from the apothecary Mr Edmund Anderson of Queen Square.

A visit to artists' studios was often a feature of a visit to Bath and the Franks went to see Thomas Beach 'the limner' or portrait painter at no. 2 Westgate Buildings; they paid 1/- which was the charge for one gentleman or two ladies to view his paintings. Beach had trained under Sir Joshua Reynolds and had come to Bath by 1770 to take advantage of the demand for portraits from the upper class visitors to the city. Horace Walpole had visited Beach's studio in 1781 to hear a concert in the picture room, a room that had been clearly designed to present the portraits on show in the best light. 'A fine light and shade being thrown upon the paintings everyone found himself surrounded, as if by magic, by a number of his acquaintances, breathing in canvas; and in such natural shapes did the pictures look upon, and seem to listen to us, that it was difficult to persuade ourselves they were not auditors also'.[68]

The week following the visit to Beach the Franks spent 4/- visiting the studios of both Beach and Mr William Hoare, the cost suggesting that Jacob, Priscilla and Abigail all viewed the paintings.[69] Hoare was the senior portrait painter in Bath having settled in the city in 1739 and remained so until Thomas Gainsborough appeared on the scene in 1759. Hoare played an important role in the city in addition to his painting as he was a supporter and one time Governor of the Mineral Water Hospital that had been opened in 1742. Churchgoing was another divertissement and a payment to the clerk of the Octagon, a private subscription chapel behind Milsom Street meant the Franks could attend church services in a socially exclusive private chapel.

The stay in Bath ended on the 27th January 1785. The waiters of the Upper Rooms had been sent their 'Xmas Box' on the 28th December and the

68   Sloman, Susan Legouix, (1996) 'Artists' Picture Rooms in Eighteenth Century Bath, Bath History, Vol. VI, p. 135.

69   Thomas Beach 1738-1806, and William Hoare of Princess Street, 1707-1792 both painted portraits of Bath's wealthy visitors. Thicknesse, op cit, pp. 48-49. Beach's ticket prices, Bath Chronicle.14/5/1778.

cook and maid at the lodgings were each tipped one guinea before the Franks party left the city. In the margin of the cash book for the last day in Bath there is a small note 'Lost £21-5s-6d', was this gambling losses? Gambling was such a common aspect of a visit to Bath that it would be surprising if the Franks were not playing cards in the Assembly Rooms; and as we have seen an interpretation of the word 'play' could mean that gambling had been part of their visits since the first one. If they had been gambling however the stakes they played for seem relatively small compared with the fortunes that could be won or lost in the Assembly Rooms and York House. There is an entry in the cash book for two guineas paying for 'arrears at the club'; what club this was is obscure. There are references in the nineteenth century to a York Club so perhaps Jacob had joined a predecessor club and perhaps went there to play cards.

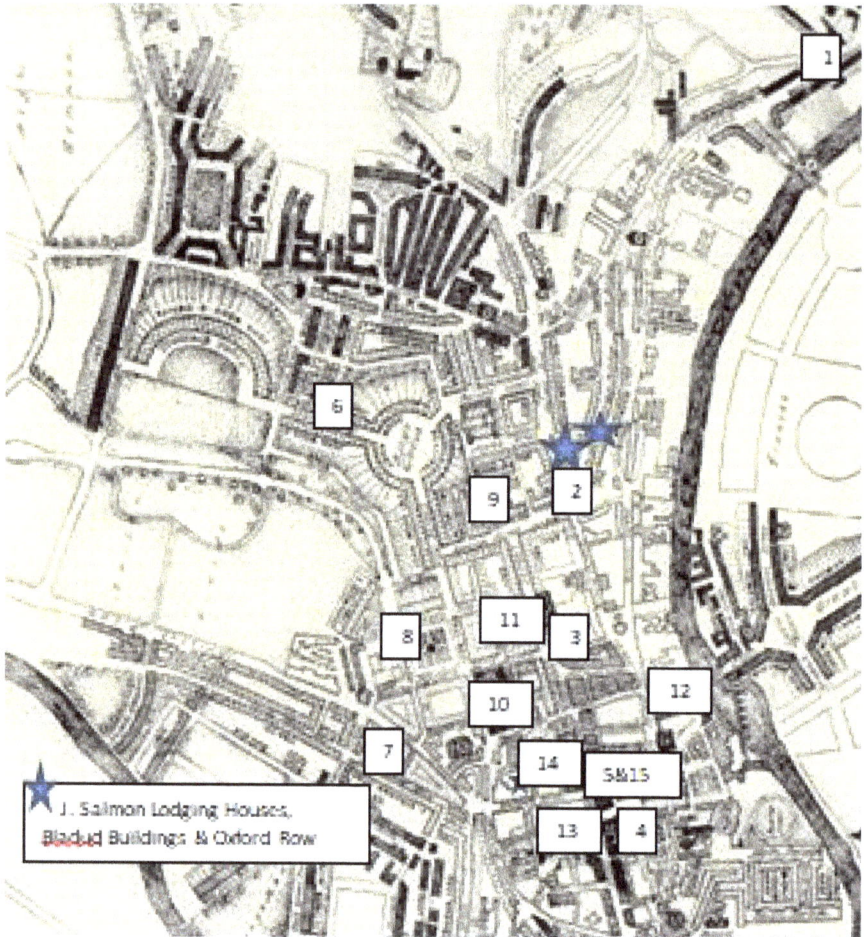

1. Walcot Porter Brewery, 2. Henry Derham's wine vaults, Fountain Buildings 3. William Basnett, goldsmith, Bond St. 4. Christopher Marsh, woollen draper, Abbey Yard, 5. Arthur Jones woollen draper, Cheap St. 6. George Sheid, grocer, Brock St. 7. J. Croome, coal merchant New King St., 8. Edmund Anderdon, apothecary, Queen Square, 9. Thomas Wilson, 'mans mercer' St Andrew's Terrace, 10. J. Taylor, hairdresser, Trim St. 11. Mollands confectioners, Milsom St. 12. Thomas Parsons, breeches maker, Northgate St. 13.White Hart Inn, Stall St. 14. Bear Inn, Stall St. & Union Passage,15. Minifie, Cheese monger, Cheap Street.

The Tradesmen supplying the Franks at Bath: author's collection

6

Bored with Bath?

The years of not visiting the city?

THERE WAS NEARLY a twenty year gap until the next entries in the cash book record a visit to Bath in March 1803. Had the Franks simply grown bored of Bath; although it was still a popular resort it was past its glory days of Beau Nash and Royal visits. It is of course possible that the Franks had been to Bath in the intervening years but had simply kept their accounts in a different book, perhaps having mislaid the one that has however survived in the archives.

Indeed it seems probable that the Franks did visit Bath between 1784 and 1803. The 'arrivals' pages of the *Bath Chronicle* records the arrival of Mr and Mrs Franks in April 1786 and in November 1787, the visits of two Mr Franks, together with a Mrs Franks, in November and December 1788[70] and a Mr & Mrs in December 1789. A further visit of a Mr Franks was reported in March 1790.[71] Of course it is not possible to be certain that any of these Mr and Mrs Franks were Jacob and Priscilla. However in the May of 1788 a Mr Franks made a benefaction of three guineas to the Bath Hospital, depositing

The Hot Bath: courtesy of Akeman Press.

70   *Bath Chronicle*s arrivals section (p.3), 8/11/1787, 20/11/1788, 24/12/1788, Hot Bath Pump Room, 1/5/1788, p1.

71   *Bath Chronicle* arrivals section, 18/3/1790, p.3.

the money at the Hot Bath Pump Room (also known as the Hetling Pump Room) next to the Hot Bath. As shall be seen in his 1803 visit Jacob Franks was probably having 'dry pumping' treatment at the Hot Bath increasing the probability that the Mr Franks at the Hot Baths Pump Room in 1788 was Jacob Franks.

THE HETLING PUMP ROOM AND THE HOT BATH

The Hot Bath designed by John Wood the Younger was completed in 1777 to provide a more comfortable place for fashionable people to bathe in the hot mineral water. In the late 1770s the Bath Corporation bought the adjacent Hetling Pump Room from Ernest Hetling who had been running it since 1749 as somewhere to drink the water as a complement to the bathing provided in the new Hot Bath. The Pump Room had been refurbished by 1788. The Corporation employed Thomas King, a marble mason, to remove all the old fittings and replace them with a new marble basin, a marble vase and a carved wooden case for the pump. Repairs were also made at the Cross Bath including 'setting in pluggs' to two water closets in 1785.[72] There was another set of up-market bathing facilities known as the New Private Baths located between the Kings Bath and Stall Street that were designed by Thomas Baldwin and completed in 1778.

In 1803 the Franks were back in Bath and took up the cash book again and new entries were made following seamlessly after the old ones. By that time however the costs of visiting Bath had considerably increased as the value of the pound had almost halved, and in 1800 the inflation rate had been 36%. There were several causes;[73] the Napoleonic War had consumed huge quantities of food, fuel and military materiel causing shortages and prices to rise. These increases were exacerbated by an increasing population which further increased demand for diminishing supplies. In the north of England where industrial production had expanded wages kept level with price increases, but in Bath

72   Chamberlain's accounts (uncatalogued) Voucher and receipt from Thomas King for work done between 13th April and 23rd September 1785, bill paid 11th October 1788. Bath Record Office.

73   Gregory, J. (2022), Untold Lives Blog; 'The cost of living crisis, part 2, inflation in 1800'. 12/5/2022, British Museum.

between 1780 and 1801 real wages halved.[74] For visitors like the Franks this would have eased the cost of hiring servants and other services in the city. At a national average level though the pound in 1810 was still the cost of six day's labour by a skilled workman as it had been in 1780.

74   Neale, op cit,p. 86.

7

TAKING THE CURE:
BATH, SPRING SEASON 1803

When Jacob and Priscilla Franks came to Bath at the end of March 1803 the focus of the visit changed; the Assembly Rooms were no longer quite the centre of their activities, instead it was the hot mineral water baths. After a few nights at the White Hart they rented no. 36 Milsom Street from Mrs Thomas for 8 guineas a week. They brought at least three of their servants with them, certainly John Freilick the butler, Sarah Liversedge and William Argent, who was often paid for buying 'sundries', the latter two were with the Franks on previous excursions.

The change in emphasis in their activities was most likely a consequence of ill health; the Franks were in their mid to late 50s and one or other of them was ill. It was probably Jacob Franks who was in poor health; when he died in 1814 the cause was described as 'gout of the stomach' and the Doctor Gibbes whom the Franks consulted in Bath was a specialist in gout as well as a published author of two treatises on the curative efficacy of the Bath mineral waters. There are several enigmatic entries in the cash book early in the visit for 'bathing tubs'. Possibly the tubs of hot mineral water were brought to the Jacob's lodgings. In 1864 an advertisement for the Pump Room & Bath offered:

> PORTABLE BATHS filled with Mineral Waters at a temperature not exceeding 106°, can be supplied at any short distance. – Slipper and Hip Baths at 1s 6d per week; Tubs of Water, 1s each.[75]

Such service was probably available much earlier than 1864. One entry in the book mentions a 'bathing tub & ice' suggesting Jacob was trying a different sort of bathing treatment at home to alleviate his condition. Perhaps as a subscriber to the New Assembly Rooms he took advantage of the cold

---

75 Wright, G. N. (1864) *The Historic Guide to Bath*, Bath: Peach, advertisement section at end of book.

plunge pool available in the basement of the Rooms for the use of members. He also purchased opodeldoc for half a crown which was an alcoholic liniment and a treatment for gout that sometimes contained laudanum.[76] Then the cash book records the fees for 18 treatments of 'dry pumping' and two sessions of 'bathing'. Bathing clearly implies full immersion in the hot mineral water but dry pumping refers to localised treatment whereby the hot water was pumped and directed only towards the ailing part of the body. Jacob Franks had the treatment nearly every day of his stay and the entry for the 13th April has a short notation

A ghost advert in Bath for [opo] deldoc,(2nd item in list), Friars Balsam, laxatives & stomach pills: author's collection.

'Hb' suggesting that he was treated at the Hot Baths which provided dry pump rooms connected to private dressing rooms as well as access to private bathing slips and a water closet. The cost of dry pumping depended on how many strokes of the pump were made by the Pumper. The price was 6d per 100 strokes. Franks normally had 200 strokes at 1/- but on the 25th April this was raised to 400 and two days later to 600, costing 3/-. Dry pumping at the Hot Bath was nearly twice as expensive as the same treatment at the King and Queen's Baths.[77] Between the last two sessions Jacob took a 9d 'emulsion' although which of the many medical emulsions available it was is not known. The pumper was given a tip of 7/- at the end of the course of treatment and 'Old Norris'[78] the guide at the baths who oversaw gentlemen's

76   The advertisement for opodeldoc is discussed in Swift, A. & Elliott, K. (2016) *Ghost Signs of Bath*, Akeman Press, p. 89. The advert is on the wall of the Porter restaurant at the corner of George Street and Miles Buildings.

77   In his 1813 guide John Feltham records the price of dry pumping at the Kings & Queens Baths as 4d per 100 strokes and 6d per 100 strokes in both the Hot Bath and the new private baths that were adjacent to the King's Bath. Feltham, J. (1813) *A guide to the watering and sea-bathing places*, London: Longman, p.37. That Franks was paying 6d per 100 strokes increases the likelihood that he was receiving the treatment at the Hot Bath but it remains a possibility that it was at the New Private Baths that were built between Stall Street and the King's Bath in 1789.

78   From Graham's *New Treatise on Bath Waters*, 'Next morning the patient is carried into the bath… and exults in the soothing and most comfortable influences…

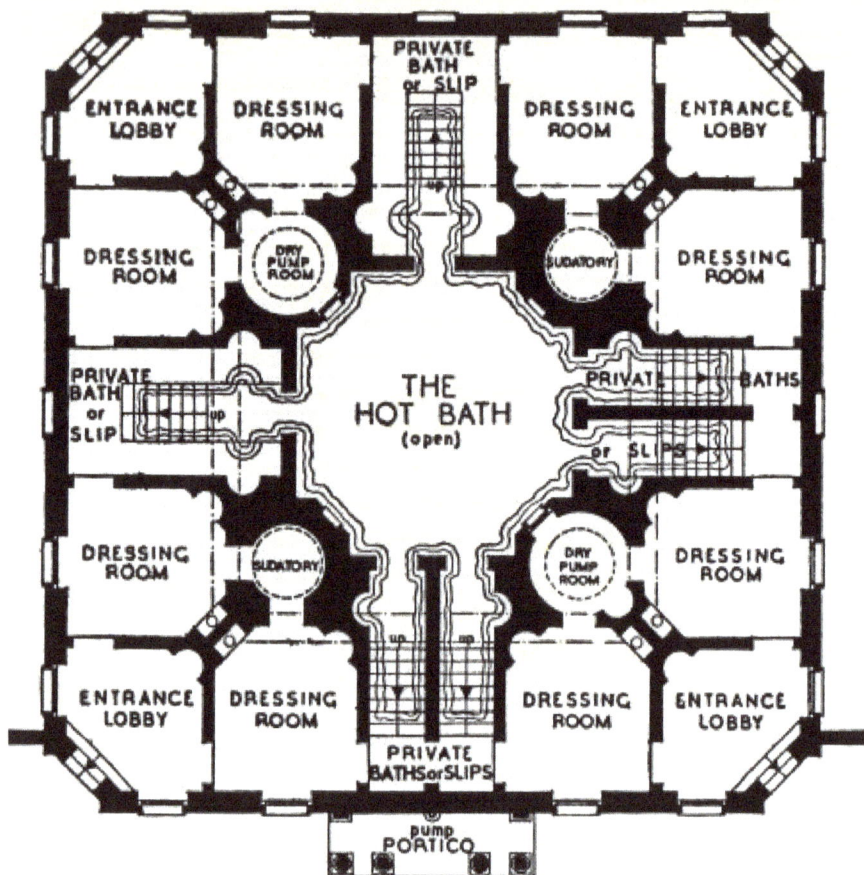

The internal layout of John Wood the Younger's Hot Baths: author's collection.

immersion in the hot water was also given a tip.

Taking the air seems to have been part of Dr Gibbes' prescription because there are many references to 'trnpkes', an abbreviation for the tolls on turnpike roads, which together with the purchase of a Bath Guide book and a map of 'Around Bath' suggests that one or both Franks went on excursions, having an 'airing', in the countryside beyond the city. There were bills for hiring and stabling two horses and on the 28th April the Franks had the problem of having to sack their groom for drunkenness.

"But Mr Norris" shouts the chairman "Master's time is up". "Sir" says the guide" you must rise your time is up, you have been in ten minutes" '. 1789, quoted in Fawcett, T. ed. (1995) *Voices of Eighteenth Century Bath*, p. 48.

The next day the Franks hired two pairs of horses and had a trip to Clifton and 'K':Weston', this was Kings-weston House and Park - a well-known beauty spot and a popular excursion from Bath. Kingsweston was another house designed by Vanbrugh. They dined (and possibly stayed) at the Royal York Hotel. Jane Austen's fictional characters the Thorpes and James Morland dined there in the novel *Northanger Abbey*. A contemporary directory of Bristol said the hotel was 'extremely well calculated for parties who arrive here, or to make excursions for a few days at this delightful spot'.[79] At that time there was a New Hotwells spa that replaced the old Hotwells inconveniently at the foot of the Avon Gorge. The New Hotwells was located where the Avon Bridge Hotel now stands.

Dr Gibbes in his writings recommended consuming less alcohol and rich food as a treatment for gout but the Franks continued to visit Molland's the Milsom Street confectioners, as they had on previous visits, and also to buy cheeses and cream cheeses, from Hemmings and from John Minifee, the cheese monger of No. 9 on the south side of Cheap Street, and sending them as gifts to all their friends and family outside of Bath. Peach, a Victorian publisher in Bath says Bath cheese was a renowned delicacy and was 'of a soft buttery consistency made from new milk and is a very pleasant, wholesome and digestible morsel'.[80] A Mr Crumden and a 'W.D.' were each

Entrance front elevation of Kings Weston House, Bristol. By Sir John Vanbrugh: Yale Center for British Art, Paul Mellon Collection.

sent a cheese and Mrs Spilsbury received a cream cheese. The identity of Mrs Spilsbury is uncertain but a possible candidate is Rebecca Spilsbury (d.1812) the wife of the engraver, painter and miniaturist Johnathan Spilsbury who was an associate of William Blake.[81] She and Johnathan had connections with

---

79   LaFaye, Deidre (2010) 'Jane Austen and Bristol' in M. J. Crossley Evans (ed.) "A *Grand City" Life, Movement and Work: Bristol in the Eighteenth and Nineteenth Centuries*, The Bristol and Gloucestershire Archaeological Society, p.189.

80   Peach, R. E. M. (1893) *Street Lore of Bath*, Bath: Blackett, p.152.

81   Davies, Keri (2006/7) 'Johnathan Spilsbury and the Lost Moravian History of William Blake', *Blake: An Illustrated Quarterly*, Winter 2006/7, pp. 102 & 107. Johnathan Spilsbury owned a house in Seymour Street in Bath, Will

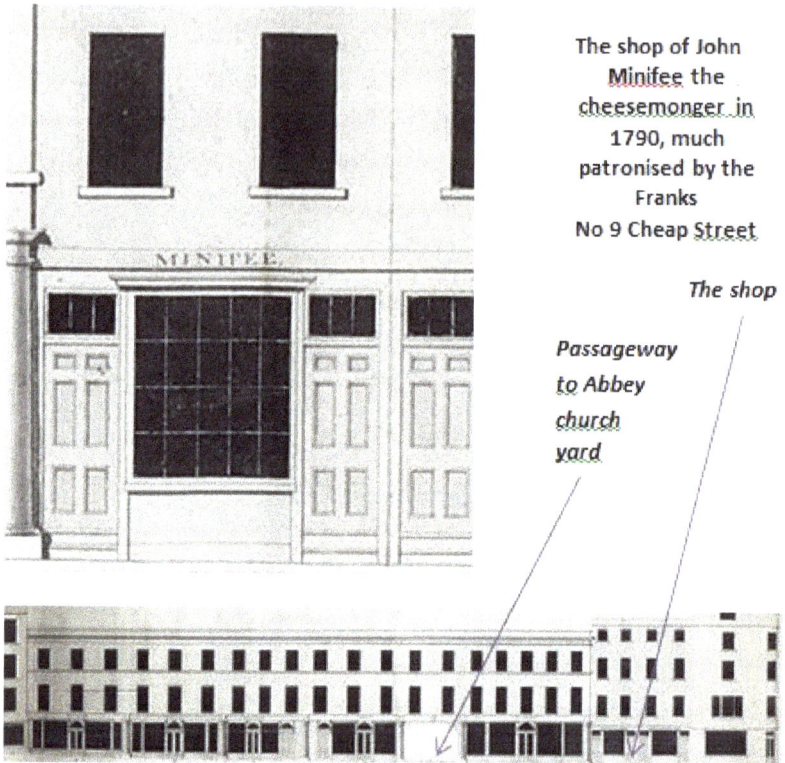

The shop of John Minifee the cheesemonger in 1790, much patronised by the Franks
No 9 Cheap Street

The shop

Passageway to Abbey church yard

Minifee the cheese monger: permission of Bath in Time.

Bath and Bristol but mainly lived in London. David Vanderheyden another recipient of food gifts was sent a 'Fowl pye' from Molland's as well as a cheese. He was an elderly neighbour living in Isleworth who had spent much of his career in India where, until 1784 when he and his wife returned to Britain, he was a contractor managing the maintenance of two large army cantonments at Berhampore and Dinapore, as well as probably having other enterprises. Later in London he ran a business[82] importing goods from India and helping

of Johnathan Spilsbury of St George's Square, London, probate 13/3/1813, PROB 11/1543/55, National Archives / Ancestry.co.uk. Another candidate is Dorothy Spilsbury of Soho Square, London the widow of Francis the inventor of Spilsbury's Antiscorbutic Pills.

82   David Vanderheyden's brother was also a merchant who operated out of Albany in New York and was involved in the ginseng trade. There was a great demand for the root in China and its supply chain stretched across eastern and western British colonies. The root was foraged by the Iroquois tribe in the Mohawk valley then sold to local traders on the frontier who then sold it to merchants

East India Company officials remit their money to Britain.[83] In 1799 he and Jacob Franks, along with many others had written a character reference to the Middlesex Magistrates supporting their local turnpike tollhouse keeper who had been convicted, unfairly they thought, of assaulting traveller.[84]

FOOD, DRINK AND OTHER SHOPPING WHILE IN BATH

There is more evidence of the Franks' food purchases while in Bath during this visit. The list includes staple items, hung beef, quarter of lamb, potatoes, broccoli and baked apples but also more indulgent items: honey, asparagus, aromatic (balsamic?) vinegar, cayenne pepper, Fry's cocoa and two doz. bottles of Madeira, as well as a key for the dram case. They bought their other wine from Mr Stroud and their beer from William Clark the brewer.

Jacob Franks returned to Parsons of Northgate Street for a new pair of breeches and for an old pair to be cleaned. Gaiters were bought from Frederic Albrecht who was a stay maker; whale bone was also purchased, probably for Priscilla's bodices. Twelve 'bordered Scotch cambric handkerchiefs' were got from Sayers costing 3/- each. Among other items he acquired during his stay Jacob bought a 'false tail'. At that time gentlemen's wigs had a short pony tail known as a queue, a false tail was a queue on a piece of thin string that could be tied around the head under a hat avoiding the necessity of wearing a wig. Various items of clothing were bought for the servants: a waistcoat for Freilick, a neckerchief for Henry, a dressing waistcoat for William, a gown for his wife. These last two were probably William and Mary Argent long time servants of the family. William, who may have been the William who was with the Franks on their tour of the north in 1778, was left an annuity in Jacob's will and Mary, when a

such as Dirk Vanderheyden. They in turn shipped it to London from where it was exported to China on East India Company ships. It was not however part of the Company's official trade but was shipped by Company officials as part of their allowance of private cargo space on the East Indiamen. Cash, S. G.(2018) 'Roots in the Valley: Ginseng and the New York-Iroquois Borderlands 1752-1785', *New York History*, Vol 9, No. 1, pp 7-37, p. 32.

83   *Calcutta Gazette*, 18/3/1784, 1/4/1784, 10/10/1793.

84   History of Parliament Online (n.d.) Vanderheyden, David, (c1758-1828), www. historyofparliamentonline.org/volume/1790-1820/member/vanderheyden-david-1758-1828.

widow, was left a bequest and annuity in Priscilla's will. The Franks
purchased a parapluie and had their travelling trunks mended.

The Assembly Rooms were not entirely neglected during the Franks'
stay in the city. Soon after their arrival they paid the ½ guinea subscription at
both Upper and Lower Rooms and on the 27th March they made an additional
subscription to the Lower Rooms, but what this paid for is not known. It was
to the Upper Rooms however that they went to a Dress Ball the following
Monday evening, the usual day for Dress Balls. The cash book also records for
that day 'Card Assembly Mrs King - 5/-'. This is the first explicit reference in
the book to playing cards and probably refers to a private party in the house of
Mrs King, the Master of Ceremonies wife, the 5/- would have been the tips for
the servants who provided the packs of cards; and who were also customarily
entitled to the stubs of candles at the end of the evening which they could sell
in the market.

LADIES CARD PARTIES AT BATH

A letter to the *Bath Chronicle* purportedly from a servant
complaining that the ladies at a house card party were too
mean with their tips is probably a satirical pastiche. The contrived
phonetic spelling of a servant's uneducated speech (contrasted with
genuinely eighteenth century exuberant punctuation) and above all
a sophisticated word play on 'brim' which meant both an abandoned
woman or prostitute (which he accused the ladies of being) and
similarly something which has lost its value, in this case dodgy money,
suggests that the following letter was not written by an uneducated
servant.[85]

Sir; Noing as how you bee a good natur'd gentleman, I hope you will
forgive the liberty I take in riting you a few lines and begs you will
finde rome for um in your next paper – you must no as I bee a poor
servant man, I has a good place, loe wages enuff, and I depend of my
parkiftes [perquisites or perks]: won part is from card-munney. Mi
mistress sees a deale of company and we had a rare doing, in the
passun weake, for all the ---- and ----. I scorne to be a blab, or else
I cud let a cat out of the bag, but I bee no tale-bearer, not I; so as

85   *Bath Chronicle*, 30/4/1795, p.2.

I was saying, my ganes cum from what the gentry pays at the card tables; but then I find wax candles, and cards, and mi mistress does not allow me the ends of um for she burns em close when we as no company; but I thinks to make a new bargin, for I takes up every nite a grate parsell of bad munney – all brims. My feller servants says, an how it is the brims who puts it there. Now is it not a shame for ladis, fine ladis, barrownites ladis, to think to starve a poor servant so! I do assure you Mister printer, I took up five from under won candlestick** last nite, not worth won fardon. I hope, if any of the ladis who does such durty trix, sees this, they will consider how hard it is upon us, who work ard for our bredd, and sometimes, and often, sum of them forgets to put down tare munney at aul: and if mistress was not to look sharp sumtimes, more woud do so. I ope the gentlefolk will take the int and not wrong us poor sarvants anymore. So no more at present, from your umble sarvant.

John Green, Crescent Bath April 27th. 1795

**One of a footman's perks was known as vails; the footman would provide the playing cards and the players would put a shilling under the candlestick as a tip.

The only other balls specifically mentioned in the cash book are the benefit balls for Mr Tyson who was then the Master of Ceremonies of the Upper Rooms and Mr James King Master of Ceremonies of the Lower Rooms. Tyson's ball was on the 11th April and Mr King's on the 15th.

Music continued to play a part in the Franks' amusements in the city and many of the concerts were held in the Assembly Rooms. They went to Rauzzini's Spring Benefit Concert on the 13th April at the Upper Rooms and to Mr Doyle's benefit at the Lower Rooms on the 20th of the month. There were however alternative venues to hear music and the Franks joined the Bath Harmonic Society which organised concerts and choral singing of 'glees and catches'. It had been founded in 1799 by the Rev John Bowen of Portland Place in the city.[86] There was a family connection, General Henry Johnson was the husband of Jacob Franks' sister Rebecca and a steward and sometime Vice-President of the Harmonic Society. The Franks went to a 'A Harmonic Supper'

86   Burnim, Kalman A. *The Letters of Sarabond William Siddons to Hester Lynch Piozzi in the John Ryland's Library*, footnote, p.80. Warner in his 'Bath Characters' satirises Bowen as Rev Bow-wow who is indecent, scurrilous and bibulous.

The Sydney Gardens, the booths in which tea was taken
can be seen in the distance on the right: courtesy of
Akeman Press.

on the 23rd March and on the 18th April to a 'Ladies Harmonic Breakfast'
at Sidney Gardens hosted by the 'Nobility and gentlemen' of the Society'.
Breakfast was on the table at 11.30 am and dancing commenced at 1pm. The
Sydney Gardens pleasure grounds were an obvious spring attraction and the
Franks paid the 6d entrance fee to explore the grounds on the 30th March. The
Assembly Rooms of course remained a good place to take tea and socialise and
at the end of the stay the waiters at the Lower and Upper Rooms were tipped
10/6d and the porters 5/.

The theatre was still important to the Franks and they saw several plays
during their stay in the city. They bought three tickets on the 21st April for
Richard Sheridan's play 'Pizarro', which had first been performed in Bath in

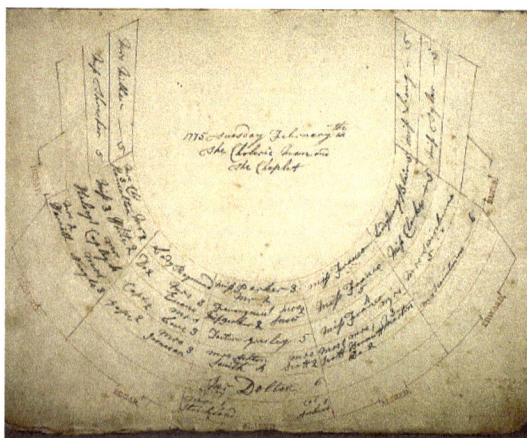

A page from the theatre box-keeper's book: permission
of Bath in Time.

1799. During this stay in Bath they mostly took seats in the boxes at the Theatre Royal which meant they had to give tips to the Box book-keeper and the Box book-keeper's boy; though on one evening in March they spent 10/6d on tickets for the pit for their servants and in April they bought Henry, another of the servants, a theatre ticket for 1/6d.

Sermons in the eighteenth century provided another form of dramatic entertainment and it seems the Franks attended Anglican churches regularly. On one occasion the Franks went to a charity sermon. During their stay pew openers, the guides who led people to their pew, were given tips on three occasions. One of these was the pew opener at St James's church. The vicar Richard Warner was a popular, if sometimes controversial, preacher but the Franks were not in Bath the following spring when he gave a sermon arguing that war was unchristian, much to the annoyance of many of his congregation. He was also an antiquarian and an anonymous writer of satires of Bath society.

There were fees paid to the library for 'Mrs F' and a copy of the 'Bath Guide' was bought. One odd entry in the cash book refers to a shilling given to the 'boy at the iron rail way' so perhaps Jacob and Priscilla had taken a walk on the 22nd April to the quarries at Combe Down and visited the gravity railway that Ralph Allen had built to bring stone from the quarries down to the wharf on the river. It was a common walking excursion from the town.

The gravity railway bringing the quarried stone down to the wharf on the river: Yale Center for British Art, Paul Mellon Collection.

A few days earlier Jacob had hired a sedan chair to visit Mr Temple, this was almost certainly Richard Godman Temple who as well as having a house at no. 7 The Circus owned a substantial country estate at Roehampton in Surrey.[87] Temple was a Unitarian and a philanthropist who died in Bath in

87   Ed Pope's History, (website) (n.d.) Temple, Richard Godman', https://

1830. Isleworth is not far from Roehampton and he and Franks would have known each other as county gentlemen.

The Franks' experience of Bath during this stay differed from that of their visits in 1777 and 1784; the Assembly Rooms had no longer such a central role as previously. Whether this was a reflection of Bath's role as a fashionable city changing or a reflection of the Franks' greater age is unclear. Getting older certainly made the Franks' more concerned with health and domestic comfort, reflected in the accounts for example by entries for smelling salts, apothecaries bills and for hiring a bidet from Mr Evill the Milsom Street auctioneer and upholsterer. Jacob and Priscilla Franks left Bath on the 5th May 1803.

edpopehistory.co.uk/entries/temple-richard-godman. Davis, V. D. (1932) *A History of Manchester College*, London: George Allen & Unwin, p. 100.

8

TAKING THE SCENIC ROUTE:
THE FRANKS RETURN TO ISLEWORTH

JACOB AND PRISCILLA did not return immediately to their home in Richmond but decided to do a tour of Hampshire on their way. The first stop on the trip was Salisbury. Of course they visited the cathedral and paid the pew opener 2/6d and a similar amount to 'a man at the cathedral'. They seldom missed an opportunity to visit a grand country house and so they hired a pair of horses and saddles and rode out to Wilton House only a few miles outside of Salisbury. It was the seat of the Dukes of Pembroke and in 1803 it was undergoing a major rebuilding project, in a Gothic style, under the direction of the architect James Wyatt. As usual the porter was tipped 3/6d to give them access and the house-keeper showed them around for a gratuity of 8/-. Like other grand houses Wilton had a catalogue of its treasures that the Franks bought a copy of for 1/6d. After leaving Salisbury they travelled into Hampshire and arrived at Winchester on the 8th May and stayed one night. They saw the cathedral and wandered around the medieval buildings and park lands of Winchester College that had been founded in 1382. Their next destination was Southampton where they put up at the Star Inn. Each place they stayed at they had to tip the waiter, the chamber maid and the boot boy who cleaned their shoes.

In Southampton they went bathing, at a cost of 5/-; this probably refers to the new fashion for sea bathing rather than mineral water bathing and this is the first mention of it in the cash book. Sea bathing and the seaside had been gaining popularity since the middle of the eighteenth century. Doctors had begun to advocate its supposed medical benefits and people began to appreciate the coast's scenic values. On a philosophical level the sea was seen as sublime, fearful in its extent and force, and invigorating in ways that contrasted with the quotidian smallness of town life. Southampton began to develop as a spa in 1750 when the Prince of Wales visited to sea bathe. It was still fashionable in the 1800s; Jane Austen and family visited between 1806 and 1809. But

John Feltham in his 1803 book *A Guide to the Watering and Sea Bathing Places* did not rate it for sea bathing. He wrote there were no bathing machines, the beach was not favourable to immersion and the saline sea water was too much mixed with fresh riverine water, in short the water, nor indeed he thought, the climate, were sufficiently bracing and sublime. Nevertheless fashionable people continued to sea bathe at Southampton.

Netley Abbey, 1814, by Amos Green: Yale Center for British Art, Paul Mellon Collection.

Near Southampton Water were the ruins of Netley Abbey,[88] a Cistercian monastery that had been sold as a mansion during the dissolution of the monasteries but had been abandoned and fallen into ruin since the early eighteenth century. By 1803 it was enjoying a tourist fame as a romantic, Gothic ruin of the kind favoured by the adherents of the Picturesque Movement. Richard Warner the vicar of St James's in Bath wrote a Gothic Story published in 1795 titled 'Netley Abbey' that featured wicked barons, mysterious skulduggery and phantoms. Perhaps the Franks had read it while in Bath as it was by one of the local vicars. The Franks consequently visited Netley

88   Hampshire Cultural Trust, https://collections.hampshireculture.org.uk/object/print-engraving-ruins-netley-abbey-hound-hampshire-drawn-1761-engraved-r-b-godfrey-published

and gave 1/3d to the boy who showed them around. From Southampton they moved on to Portsmouth which was an important naval port and they stayed two nights. Here their tourism took a nautical turn and they explored the Gun Wharf where the Royal Navy stored its ordnance, and harbour and then went sailing off Spithead where Royal Naval Reviews were held.

On the 13th May the Franks started off on the London Road towards Isleworth. That evening they dined and slept at Demezey's at Hartfordbridge.[89] This was otherwise known as the White Lion coaching Inn and was run by Nick Demezey,[90] obviously a well-known character because the inn was universally known just by his name. It had had its moment of fame the previous September when the four princesses, Augusta, Sophia, Elizabeth and Mary, on their way to Windsor from Weymouth, the Royal family's favourite seaside resort, had dined at Demezey's. The princesses' journey had caused much excitement, the garrison troops at Winchester had lined the street as they passed and the church bells had rang out, and when they stopped to change horses at Romsey the Steward of Lady Palmerston presented the princesses with a basket of fruit. After leaving Demezeys the princesses arrived at Windsor that evening in 'perfect health'. The Franks in their turn arrived home at Isleworth on the 14th May after their night at Demezey's. They had spent £290-15-2½d on their stay in Bath and their tour of Hampshire.

Demezey's, The White Lion, Hartfordbridge late nineteenth century: courtesy Lost Pubs Project.

89   *Hampshire Chronicle*, 6/12/1779, Demezey's is also mentioned in Jeremy Bentham's correspondence; *The Correspondence of Jeremy Bentham*, Vol I, 1752-1776, p.207. Image: The Lost Pubs Project, https://www.closedpubs.co.uk/hampshire/hartleywintney_whitelion.html

90   *The Sun*, 7/9/1802, p.3b.

9
SEA BATHING
THE TOUR OF RAMSGATE AND MARGATE, SUMMER SEASON, 1803

THE FRANKS DID not stay long at Isleworth; they decided to try sea bathing in Kent rather than Hampshire as an alternative to Bath's thermal waters and so headed for Ramsgate in Kent. They rented No. 7 Albion Place in the town from a Mr Kebell for seven weeks starting the 1st June 1803 at the cost of 7 guineas a week. They brought the servants with them including John Freilick, Jacob's butler, and J. Hughes as housekeeper who arranged for a cook and other servants; they hired furniture from Mr Cull and glasses from the grocer.

Albion Place, Ramsgate, early 1800s: courtesy Michael's Bookshop, Ramsgate.

Albion Place had been designed and built as an elegant Georgian terrace that would appeal to wealthy visitors to the town. The deed of stipulation when the terrace was built in 1791 followed the system developed by the Woods in Bath and required the buildings' front elevations to be to the same design and specified the details of the doorways, railings, pavement and roadway fronting the houses. The terms tavern, inn, coffee house or common ale house were not allowed to be used to describe the houses.[91]

Jacob and Priscilla chose the large No. 7 Albion Place because they had brought a family party with them of at least ten people whose identities can be deduced from clues in the cash book. There were several payments of one or two guineas to a Hy Johnson and a Geo. Johnson, these were almost certainly Henry Allen and George Johnson who were Jacob and Priscilla's nephews, Henry was 18 and George was 16. They were the sons of Jacob's sister Rebecca Franks and Major General Henry Johnson of the British army who had been stationed in America and had married Rebecca Franks in New York in 1782. The General was certainly in the party at Ramsgate and so probably was Rebecca.

The other certain members of the party were the Coopers – Lady Isabella Bell Cooper was Priscilla's niece, the daughter of her sister Phila and her husband Moses Franks. Isabella, like Rebecca Franks, had married a non-Jew; her husband was the Rev Sir William Cooper who had become a baronet when his father Sir Grey Cooper died in 1801. However the W. Cooper to whom small payments were made in the cash book was not Rev Sir William Henry Cooper but his son, also William Henry Cooper, born in 1788. The Rev Sir William had been the defendant in a scandalous criminal conversation and divorce case in the mid-1790s[92] and he was living in France with Lady Mary Cadogan his lover. So the Franks' party in Ramsgate most likely consisted of Jacob, Priscilla and Isabella, three teenage young men, Henry Johnson, George Johnson and William Cooper, three young girls, Mary Anne Cooper, Isabella Cooper and Elizabeth Anna Cooper, Isabella's daughters, and General and Rebecca Johnson.

91   Anon (n.d.) Albion Place: the deed of stipulation, www.eastcliff. co.uk?AlbionPlace2.html.

92   Confirmation that the William Henry Cooper who married Isabella Bell Franks is the same man as the one involved in the Cadogan divorce scandal is made by comparing the marriage certificate that records that the Rev William Henry Cooper married Isabella Bell Franks by special license at the house of his father Sir Grey Cooper 21/5/1787 (Ancestry.co.uk: London Metropolitan Archives) with the newspaper report that identifies the Rev William Henry Cooper, son of Sir Grey Cooper as the defendant in the Cadogan Criminal Conversation case, Saunders Newsletter & Daily Advertiser, 19/6/1794, p. 1.

The Rev William Henry Cooper's affair had created great public interest. His father Sir Grey Cooper of Worlington Park in Suffolk was a politician and a one-time Chief Secretary to the Treasury. He had revived the baronetcy to become 3rd baronet although many thought the baronetcy had never existed or that if it had Grey Cooper did not have a claim to it, and that he had used his political influence to obtain the honour. William Henry had begun his career as a Guards officer but his father could not afford the purchase of promotion and so William Henry took holy orders and in 1787 in Marylebone he married Isabella Bell Franks. The couple had a gentleman's income but no wealth. He had £500 pa as rector of Rochester and a small income as the legal custodian of his mother-in-law Phila Franks who by that date had been certified insane. However he had expectations from his wealthy father-in-law Moses Franks. Unexpectedly when Moses died in 1789 he was intestate leaving his affairs in a confused state and so the extravagant William Henry found himself in financial difficulties. Lord Cadogan who was a friend of Sir Grey Cooper offered William Henry, his wife and young family the free use of apartments in his country house in Suffolk and at his London house. Lady Mary Cadogan, nee Churchill, was Cadogan's second wife and more than twenty years younger than him. They had a contented marriage until a daughter died in infancy. Mary became depressed and an invalid and she and Cadogan drifted apart. In about 1792 William Henry began an affair with Mary; her maid Farley Murray Bull would smuggle him into Mary's bedroom and then ensure they were not disturbed. The affair lasted into 1794 by when the gossip among the servants finally reached the ears of Lord Cadogan. He formally separated from Mary and the affair with William Henry Cooper continued. In March 1794 Cadogan instituted a civil court case against Cooper for Criminal Conversation. This was an action in which the plaintiff claimed damages because the defendant had lessened the value of the plaintiff's property - in this case the plaintiff's wife – by having adulterous sex with her. The judge who was appalled that a man of the cloth should so betray the man who had been his benefactor and who also had 'a beautiful young wife and family[93]' awarded Cadogan £2,000 in damages.

William Henry abandoned Isabella and his children and ran off to Abergavenny with Mary, now fully recovered from invalidity, to avoid their angry and bitter families. But Lord Cadogan's steward found the couple's hideout and Cadogan had William Henry sent to debtors' prison in Monmouth. He may well have still been in prison when Lady Cooper was in Ramsgate with the Franks. In 1796 Cadogan won lawsuits against Mary for

93   *Derby Mercury*, 19/6/1794, p. 3.

adultery and then divorced her by having a private bill passed in the House of Lords. It seems that William Henry Cooper managed to pay the damages and he and Mary went to live in France after the war between Britain and France ended with the Treaty of Amiens but when war between the countries broke out again the couple were interned at Verdun until 1814.[94] The court cases lasted from 1794 to 1796 and the details were widely publicised in the papers and subsequently they were reprinted and widely sold as pamphlets. Isabella Bell Cooper, by 1801 Lady Cooper, remained William Henry Cooper's wife, divorce was practically impossible for a woman at the time, responsible for a teenage son and three young daughters and she was no doubt reliant on friends and family such as Jacob and Isabella Franks. Priscilla and Jacob seemed to offer Lady Cooper support after the revelations of her husband's affair; perhaps that is why they invited her to Ramsgate. The Franks bought Lady Cooper and her daughters parasols, combs and a comb brush as gifts; and on the 8th September, recorded in the cash book:

> paid for Lady Cooper 1/6 , for gown for Nanny, 15/-; for ginger 'Swt::mts' [sweetmeats], £1-11s; for 2 tickets LeBas breakt at Dandelion, £1-1s; ice, 2/3; cyder, 1/8.

Nanny was probably the nurse maid who looked after the daughters who were aged between ten and thirteen years old. Breakfast at Dandelion was a public event for the benefit of Charles LeBas the Master of Ceremonies at the Margate Assembly Rooms who in 1805 would become Master of Ceremonies of the Lower Assembly Rooms at Bath. Dandelion was a Pleasure Ground a few miles outside of Margate that had been opened since the 1760s. By 1802 public breakfasts were held there twice a week and there was a band for dancing, bowls and a swing as well as 'a pretty wood and a little plantation of shrubs.[95] It was located within the grounds of a fifteenth century manor house originally called Dent-de-lion, 'that had fallen into Gothic ruin'. Its gatehouse was painted by W.J.M. Turner in 1791. *The Times* newspaper printed an account of a benefit for LeBas at Dandelion a year later than the one Isabella Cooper went to.

94   Stone, Lawrence (1993) *Broken Lives: Separation and Divorce in England 1660-1857,* Oxford: Oxford University Press, chp. 10, pp.270-279; Brun, J. P. (2013) *The Dawkins of Moggerhanger:; a Short History*, https://moggerhanger.uk/wp-content/uploads/2021/09/Dawkins-of-Moggerhanger2.pdf.

95   *Hall's New Margate and Ramsgate Guide* (1792) Ramsgate: J. Hall, pp. 22-23.

Dandelion was yesterday the great scene of a fashionable attraction. Margate, Ramsgate and Broadstairs poured forth their hosts of visitors and the road was occupied by a string of coaches, post-chaise, barouches, sociable gigs, curricles, saddle horses and all the other modes of conveyance. Nearly 700 persons were in the garden and the amusements continued an hour longer than usual. There was a most enchanting exhibition of female beauty and elegance. The venerable old towers of Dent-de-Lion never witnessed such a display of splendid activity in the earliest days of chivalry when the Gothic magnificence was at its height. The dancing was kept up with uncommon spirit at the platform.[96]

Dent de Lion, W. J. M. Turner: Yale Center for British Art, Paul Mellon Collection.

The essence of a Regency entertainment was not the entertainers – the musicians and singers - but the company, the ton, displaying themselves to each other.

The Franks' party visited Dandelion on at least two other occasions during their stay at Ramsgate. On the 20th July at the pleasure gardens they paid '12/- for [illegible] and tea'.

By 1803 Ramsgate was a well-established tourist seaside retreat; it could be easily reached from London, coaches and diligences set out for the capital every morning in the summer and returned in the evening; alternatively twice

96   *The Times*, 18/9/1804, p. 2d.

a week boats brought visitors from London. It is not known if that is how the Franks and family arrived there. The 'New Margate and Ramsgate Guide' of 1792 said of the town.

> The town is paved and lighted, has a market place lately built… near which is a good circulating library and toyshop kept by Mr Burgess… The Assembly and Card Rooms, which were built last year, front the harbour, under them are a coffee room and agreeable accommodation for parties to dine or drink in.

Ramsgate also boasted an 'extremely good Billiard room'.[97]

When the Franks first arrived they paid the 15/- membership subscription to Burgess's library that was the social centre of polite society in the town; and renewed it on the 7th September when they decided to stay an extra two weeks. They also bought a copy of the 'Ramsgate Directory' that was published by Burgess who was also a printer, as a guide for the duration of their visit. The Franks also kept four seats in the chapel and attended a charity sermon on the 21st August.

Mrs Franks, Priscilla, together with General Johnston and Lady Isabella Cooper went to a Grand Concert at the Ramsgate Assembly Rooms on the evening of 4th September at which, among other performers, Mr Weippert played the pedal harp and his daughter the piano forte. However the Company was quite small because Mrs Townley hosted one of her concerts and entertainments that same evening at Townley House which most of the 'elegant residents' of Ramsgate attended. The Franks party were clearly of the second rank of visitors to Ramsgate.[98] Mary Townley was the leading socialite in the town and also an early woman architect; she had designed the prestigious Townley House in 1792 and had also designed Albion Place where the Franks were lodging.

However the main attraction of Ramsgate was the sea. The Franks went sailing twice in July and on the 15th September sailed to the Downs to view the White Cliffs of Dover. They also went salt water bathing though whether in the 'warm salt water baths, in a very good construction'[99] or in the sea itself is unknown. Whichever, at the end of their stay they 'paid for bathing 27 times £4-17s.' and gave 'Ratcliffe bather' 14/-, likely a tip for a bathing attendant. The sea bathing machine had been invented in nearby Margate in the early eighteenth century and an account of Ramsgate in the 1830s describes upwards

97   *Hall's New Margate and Ramsgate Guide* op cit, p.48.

98   *Morning Post*, 7/9/1803, p.3b.

99   *Hall's New Margate and Ramsgate Guide*, op cit, p.42.

of twenty bathing machines operating in the season and the bathers waited in comfortable waiting rooms for their turn to use the 'cleanly and comfortable machines with careful and experienced guides' and afterwards take a walk on the parade.[100] Elizabeth 'Betsy' Sheridan in August 1788 told her sister about sea water bathing at Margate.

'The Bathing Place at Ramsgate', c1788, Benjamin West: Yale Center for British Art, Paul Mellon Collection.

At Seven I went down to the bathing House where I found a great number of Ladies and Gentlemen waiting to take their turn in the Machines which are comparatively few in number. They are much better contrived than those we had in Scarboro' [ ]. The canvas which is behind when you are at a proper depth is let down into the water and forms a compleat bath where the Guide stands to receive you. It is quite light as the Canvass is very thin. I never bathed so comfortably in my life and find myself much revived by my dip. I have settled to go before Seven every morning.[101]

100 Wyman, J. (1980) Aspects of Holidaymaking and Resort Development within the Isle of Thanet with particular reference to Margate, c1736-c1840, PhD thesis, University of Kent, pp. 76-77.

101 LeFanu (ed) (1960) *Betsy Sheridan's Journal: Letters from Sheridan's sister 1784-*

Other pastimes pursued by the Franks included sketching, drawing paper and a pencil were purchased, shooting and riding.

If the visit to Kent and its sea bathing was for health reason such a motivation might be supported by the party's medicine bill. They bought Gourlard extract, a patent remedy for inflammation, and two pints of lavender water. They spent 12/8½d at Pemberton's the druggist and £10-4s at Young's the apothecary. Jacob paid to have his head shaved a couple of times, this was more comfortable when wearing wigs.

Margate is not far from Ramsgate and the Franks and their party went there on several occasions, sometimes for the balls at Master of Ceremonies, Le Bas', Margate Assembly Rooms. Two tickets for the ball were bought on 9th August 'for W. Cooper and self', on the 15th five tickets were purchased, three on the 30th but on 7th September only one. When the Franks were about to leave Kent they gave a guinea to the Master of Ceremonies, having given him a guinea when they had first arrived. Margate also had a theatre and tickets were twice bought to see a play in August.

Meals were organised by Hughes the housekeeper and there were many payments to her for housekeeping including food. Otherwise the only mentions of food in the cash book are: a ½lb. of cocoa bought when they first arrived at Ramsgate, cakes and strawberries on visits to Margate and 'fish for water souché' [souchey]. This was a Dutch dish in origin, fish, usually perch, served in the herbed water used for boiling it, and introduced to Britain under William III. There are however plenty of entries for alcohol. On the 27th July when they had the water souchey a half dozen bottle of 'Lisbon', Portuguese white wine, were bought. (While they were in Ramsgate the Franks received a letter from Oporto raising the possibility they were involved in the wine trade. They also had a letter from Jamaica where they were involved in sugar plantations and a reminder where some of the wealth that paid for the Franks' excursions came from). Several bills from Paul Jackets the wine dealer were paid as well as 3 guineas to Abrams for other wine. A new corkscrew was purchased. At the end of the stay the brewer J. Stevenson was paid £24-18s for beer.

On the 22nd September the Franks settled up their bills, the balance of Mr Hughes' housekeeping bill was paid, Mr Kebell received the rent for the extra two weeks the party had stayed and he was given £1-15-8d for the broken china. The total cost of travelling to and from Kent was £68-15-1d. Mr Burgess was paid £2-15-6d for 9 weeks hire of a 'R[iding] horse'.[102]

1786 & 1788-1790, London: Eyre & Spottiswoode, p. 114.

102   This is a best guess reading, see the 'Indecipherable' section, appendix 3. The

10

Clubs, Societies and the Assembly Rooms

Bath, Winter Season, 1803-4

THE *Bath Chronicle* reported on the 17th November 1803 the arrival of a Mr Franks; a Miss Franks' arrival was reported on the 8th December and that of Mrs Franks on the 29th December. On their arrival in the city they bought visiting cards in preparation for their stay.

The Miss Franks was probably Abigail, Abby, Franks who had previously visited Bath with Jacob and Priscilla. Abigail never married and died in 1815 at Mortlake in Surrey. The first two bequests in her will were to Mrs and Mr Franks of Isleworth. Although her father had been a practising and committed Jew giving much to Jewish charities Abigail asked for a pious Christian burial and gave much of her money to the charity for converting Jews to Christianity.[103]

Initially the Franks stayed at a Bath inn but then rented a house from Mr R. Todd who ran a livery stable behind Queen Square and lived nearby at No. 6 Princes Street. This was a 'roomy and commodious house' and it is probably the one that the Franks took, certainly Todd occasionally let out his house, or perhaps part of it.[104] The Franks bought 2 tons 4cwt [hundredweight] of coal to warm the house at a cost of £2-2-2d plus 4d to weigh the coal. Coal supplies had to be restocked several times during their stay. The Franks had brought their usual retinue of servants with them, J. Hughes the housekeeper, Freilick the butler, Sarah Liversedge who did the laundry and Henry who ran errands. At the end of the visit Jacob paid for four places on the stage coach for their return to London.

cash book does also include payments to a farrier and a saddler.

103   Daiches-Dubens op cit p.160 and Will of Abigail Franks of Mortlake, National Archives, 4/1/1815, PROB 11/1564/37.

104   *Bath Chronicle* 15/12/1803, p.2d,, the house occupied by Mr Todd was advertised for letting in the *Bath Chronicle*, 15/12/1806, p.3d. Todd was owner of the livery stables, *Bath Chronicle*, 12/6/1806, p.3d..

As on previous visits to Bath the subscriptions to the Assembly Rooms were quickly made, but there was again a change in emphasis during this visit; clubs and societies became more important (although a brief mention of a club did figure in the cash book in 1784). On the 23rd December the cash book records payment of a subscription to 'the club'. Jacob Franks, most likely him rather than Priscilla, visited the club on at least a dozen times, during their stay sometimes for a sandwich, sometimes for a negus and sometimes for both. So the club sounds very much like a gentleman's club but identifying it is difficult. One club mentioned in the *Bath Chronicle* before 1810 is the Catch and Glee Club based in York House. This could be the club Jacob joined given that he and Priscilla were fond of music. If a contemporary satirical verse published in 1811 is to be believed the Catch Club was driven out of its home in the Long Room of York House to the Lion Inn by 'the Club', primarily a gambling club. The satirical verse claimed that Mr Reilly the manager of York House who 'turns every grain into grist / gave the Long Room to the players of Whist / T'was hard but he thought of this case in the light / Those meet once a week, and these meet once a night'.[105] If the 'club' needed more spacious accommodation for its growing membership it is likely it had existed well before 1810. Most probably this was the Bath Club, which was mentioned in the Chronicle in March 1810,[106] and is the club that most likely Jacob Franks joined. In 1814 the Bath Club hosted a masked ball at the Lower Rooms that was attended by 600 people.[107] The Bath Club is still mentioned in the newspapers in 1819 by which time there was also a York Club unsurprisingly

The York House hotel, where many clubs were based: courtesy of Akeman Press.

105   Anon (1811) *The Wonder of a Week in Bath*, London, pp.49-50.

106   *Bath Chronicle*, 15/3/1810, p.3b.

107   *Bath Chronicle*, 24/2/1814. There had been a Bath & West of England Club that

based in York House, it first appears in the papers in 1816. These two clubs probably merged but the early history of clubs in Bath is still obscure. A final but unlikely contender to be Jacob's club is the India Club that also met at York House and is first mentioned in 1806, but as its name implies, this was probably a club for those who had returned from careers in India. It may have been a predecessor of the Bath Club.

The Harmonic Society was also playing an increasing role in the Franks' musical amusements and they paid their subscriptions when they arrived back in the city. A 'Harmonic Society Ribband' was ordered on the 1st February. They attended three 'harmonic suppers' and two 'Ladies Nights' at which the gentlemen of the Society hosted the women. The one held on the 5th January was at the Lower Rooms and Jacob and Priscilla's relation Lieutenant General Johnson was the Steward, the Franks bought six tickets. The next Ladies Night was on the 8th February and the *Bath Chronicle* reported 'The second gallant fete of the Harmonic Society to the Ladies equalled the former gala in elegance, taste and liberality... it exceeded all prior entertainments of the like nature given by this body of musical amateurs'. The Franks again had six tickets. There was another Harmonic Society event on the 24th February and a Benefit for Mr Clifton who was a piano and singing teacher of St Margaret's Buildings.

THE HARMONIC SOCIETY BLUE RIBBAND

The Harmonic Society's regular evening meetings were held at the White Hart and during the first part of the evening fourteen glees would be sung, interspersed with choruses, by the best singers available in the city and they were accompanied on the pianoforte by Mr Loder. At ten o'clock a grace set to music by Wesley was sung and everyone ate a cold supper at a cost of 5/- for the food and wine. After they had finished eating Byrd's 'Non-nobis' was sung. Then up until midnight all joined in with songs and catches until proceedings ended with 'God save the King'. In 1799 the Prince of Wales had attended a meeting and had agreed to become the Society's patron and he gave permission for members to wear the Harmonic Society Ribband. It was Garter blue and featured an embroidered plume across a lyre and the Society's motto 'Curarem dolce lenimen' – cares sweet solace.[108]

was partially dissolved in 1811 leading to the formation of a breakaway club – the Kingston Club. *Bath Chronicle*, 6/2/1812.

108 Anon 'Dotted Crochet' (1908) Bath: Its musical associations, *The Musical Times*, vol. 49, 1/11/1908, pp. 695-704, p.702

The number of tickets bought for the Harmonic
Society events clearly shows that the Franks were part
of a wider party. General and Mrs Johnson who lived in
Bath were probably in their number but there was one
particular person in the party who was recorded in the
cash book as 'AH' using a monogram for the initials;
suggesting that he or she was of some significance to
the Franks. 'AH' attended the performance of Handel's 'Messiah', with Jacob
at Rauzzini's benefit concert at the New Rooms on Christmas Eve. There were
many other entries about excursions with AH including a subscription to a
ball and visits to the club. The most likely identifications of AH is Andrew
Hamilton the son of Abigail, Jacob's sister. Abigail Franks had married Andrew
Hamilton, a wealthy merchant of Philadelphia, in 1768 and their son Andrew
Hamilton was born there in 1775.[109] In 1784 Abigail's brother in law Billy
Hamilton brought his nephews the young Andrew Hamilton and his brother
James to England to go to school.[110] Abigail's husband, the boys' father, Andrew
Hamilton died in late 1784 after a long illness from which he had no hope
of recovery. A family friend wrote that it would take Abigail a long time to
recover from her grief.[111] Hamilton's will was dated December 1784, and there
is an entry in the cash book for the 15th January 1785 for 'mourning buckles',
was this when they heard of Andrew's death? Andrew and James remained in
England living with Jacob and Priscilla. So it would not be surprising if they
had brought Andrew Hamilton with them on their trip to Bath. In his will
of 1814 Jacob Franks left this Andrew Hamilton £1,000. Andrew Hamilton
married in Bath at St Swithin's in 1817 and spent most of his life in the city.

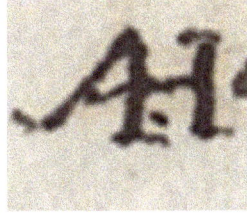

Andrew Hamilton figures as 'AH' in two other entries that refer to 'play
AH & self' that raises the question discussed earlier about whether this was a
reference to theatre going or to cards and gambling. If it meant play going they
would have seen 'The Mountaineers' and 'Bluebeard' at the Theatre Royal on
the 14th January.

It is clear however that by this visit card playing and gambling played a
bigger part in the Franks' time in Bath. In the New Year they organised their
own rout or private card party; such private and relatively informal functions
had always carried more social kudos than the public events in the Assembly

109   Private family tree for Andrew Hamilton, 1775-1825, Ancestry.co.uk.

110   Stern op cit, pp. 164,166. Preston Long, T. (1991) The Woodlands, a Matchless
      Place, Masters dissertation, University of Philadelphia, pp. 99-100, 413.

111   Jay, John, letter dated 25/11/1784, Papers of John Jay, Massachsusets Historical
      Society, ref Columbia.jay.04706, digital copy available online.

Rooms. The catering was provided by Molland's with other items from Sheid the grocer, tables and chairs were hired from Mr English.

IMPRESSING GUESTS AT A ROUT

One Mrs R------ was renowned for hiring silver plate to display on her sideboard when she was entertaining at a rout and for employing a servant to keep the parlour door open so that guests could not avoid seeing the display. A satirical poem described the situation.

> When routs her numerous friends collect,
> Her sideboard claims the first respect,
> Proving to each astonish'd guest,
> Her wealth, magnificence and taste.
> But each astonish'd guest remains,
> In doubt concerning *Ways and Means*,
> Lest envied jewels, envied plate,
> Unjust suspicions should create;
> Let it be known,
> That they in truth are, - *Not her own.*[112]

The drawing rooms at routs, often one was given to cards and an adjoining one to *converzazione* or gossip, were filled with slight acquaintances as well as friends. Tea, coffee, orgeat (almond cordial), ices and cakes would be served and the event would finish at 10pm.[113]

Cards and gambling had not featured in the cash book until spring 1803 when as we have seen Priscilla Franks attended a private card party. At the end of this winter visit the cash book records a loss at cards of £11-7s., a relatively trivial amount.

Of course social events at the two Assembly Rooms were still attended by the Franks. At the New Rooms (in all probability) the Franks paid for three tickets for the Dress Ball (one of which was for AH), and three tickets for the F[ancy] Ball (including one for Mrs F and one for AH). The Fancy Ball was

112 Gay, John, *Bath Poems* Anon (Thomas Martyn) (n.d.) Drawings from Living Models taken at Bath, bound in with other works, p.10. Bath Record Office: Local Studies Collection.

113 Fawcett, Trevor, (1998) *Bath Entertain'd*, Bath: Ruton, pp. 73-74.

new. By 1792 the popularity of the Cotillion Balls had declined and so the Masters of Ceremonies at both Rooms changed their name to Fancy Balls and modified their form.[114] Henceforward ladies would be allowed to wear hats and 'any mode of dress (that of character excepted) which they may think most elegant and becoming'. The Fancy Ball would begin with a country dance rather than the Minuet which would be followed by one cotillion only, tea would follow and then the dancing would recommence with a country dance, a cotillion, more country dances and end with a long Minuet. The Franks also paid subscriptions for the use of the Coffee Room and the Card Room. The Franks party certainly attended the Benefit Ball for Mr Richard Tyson the New Rooms' Master of Ceremonies on the 9th January and that for Mr King at the Lower Rooms on the 13th of the month. The illustration shows Mr Tyson who was also Master of Ceremonies at Tunbridge Wells hawking tickets for his Benefit Ball.[115] There was also a Cotillion Ball on the 26th January that the Franks attended.

HATS NOT TO BE WORN IN THE ASSEMBLY ROOMS

In November 1785 the Masters of Ceremonies at both Rooms were at one when it came to hats. Tyson of the Upper Rooms and King of the Lower both placed the same announcement in the Chronicle.[116]

It seems perfectly reasonable that the regulations of DRESS should be conformable to the prevalence of Fashion and accommodated to the pleasures of the LADIES, as far as the peculiar customs of Bath can warrant. Upon this principle the MASTER of the CEREMONIES always anxious to shew every mark of respect and attention to the Ladies, thinks it advisable to indulge them in their desire of coming to

114 Hunt Collection Vol. 4, p. 144, Bath Record Office, also available on Bath in Time website.

115 Dighton, Robert, (1798) Dicky Dangle the Bath and Tunbridge Wells Guide, print. Lewis Walpole Library, Yale University, call no. 798.10.00.01. The identification with Richard Tyson is confirmed in *Notes & Queries*, 3rd. Series, Vol. 10, Aug 1866, p. 155. Thanks to Tim Moore for interpreting the meaning of the caricature's title. For the definition of dangle see the *Oxford English Dictionary* (OED) and Grose, *The Vulgar Tongue*. The OED quotes a usage of 'dancing attendance' in 1704.

116 *Bath Chronicle*, 10/11/1785, p.3d.

the Rooms on *Sunday* and *Tuesday* evenings in hats, that are expected in some degree ornamented, otherwise it will induce the necessity of again prohibiting them – But *It must be observed*, that hats of *no sort* will be allowed either at the *Concerts, or Cotillion or Dress balls,* and if any lady should through inattention, or other motive, infringe this regulation, she must not take it amiss, if she should be obliged to take off her hat, or quit the Assembly.

In 1780 there had been an incident reported[117] by Edmund Rack when the Master of Ceremonies of the Upper Rooms had threatened to remove a lady's hat himself.

Capt. Dawson Master of Ceremonies [of the New Rooms] & the Bishop of Worcester's Lady had lately a dispute on dress at ball night. The lady came in with a hat on, which is contrary to the established rules. Capt. D politely remonstrated – the lady would not obey. The Capt. insisted – she would not but retired to the tea room. The Capt. follow'd her, & told her that if she would not comply, disagreeable as the task would be, he must be oblig'd to take her hat off himself. She was still obstinate and ordering her [sedan] chair left the Rooms. The conduct of Capt. D was highly applauded, but the Bishop has been silly enough to resent it, & some abusive letters have appeared in the London papers on the occasion.

DICKY DANGLE DANCE.
The BATH & TUNBRIDGE WELLS Guide.

Dicky Dangle Dance: Courtesy Lewis Walpole Library, Yale University   Dicky is short for Richard, dangle is an old term for a person who attaches themselves to someone, dallies and 'dances attendance' on them, in the hope of an advantage, such as selling a ticket for a benefit ball.

117   Rack, Edmund, *A Disultory Journal of Events in Bath*, op.cit. 22/1/1780.

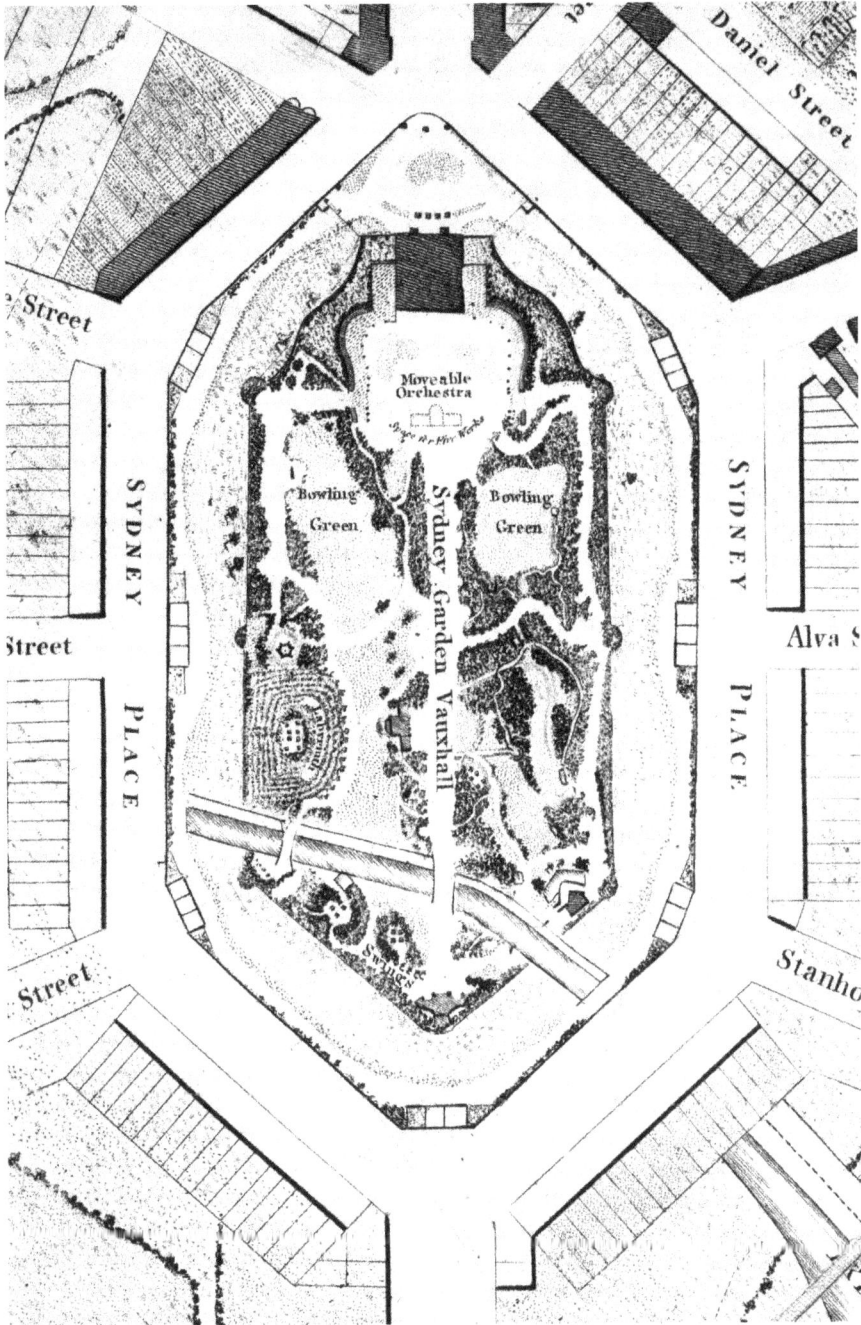

Sydney Gardens 1800, showing the 'Ride' around the pleasure grounds: Bath in Time.

Concerts at the Rooms were still an important part of the Franks' social round. They were at the eleventh of the subscription series of concerts at the New Rooms on the 1st February and hired a chair to go home; and on the 22nd February at the New Rooms they attended a concert directed by Rauzzini to benefit the Bath City Dispensary and Asylum for the Sick Poor. The waiters and porters at both sets of Rooms were given their usual tips over the Christmas period. As he walked around the city Jacob Franks often passed a destitute 'old man' and on at least five occasions gave him a shilling.

Visits to Molland's the coffee house figured much during this winter season, and the waiters and porters there were given a good tip, but tea was also taken at the Lower Rooms, the Upper Rooms and the club. There were other occasional treats such as the purchase of honey, apples occasionally, oranges frequently, a pint of raspberries, a pint of orange ice, iced cakes, 'spunge' biscuits, rose essence, many lozenges, one and a half dozen bottles of expensive ''ho'ryean' (haut brion) claret from Bordeaux and a bottle of champagne. The Franks also spent £2-5-2d on new china at William Ellen's china and glassware shop that until 1792 had been Wedgwood's shop in Milsom Street managed by William Ward.[118] Bath had good bookshops and an atlas was purchased. The Franks also, as they had during previous visits, regularly sent cheeses bought from Minifee the cheesemonger to friends and relations including to Mrs Spilsbury. One friend, David Vanderheyden (who had received the fowl pie the previous spring) was sent a haunch of venison and later a joint of lamb. This was perhaps to be shared with David Vanderheyden jnr. who had recently returned from his twenty five year long career as an East India Company official. He would become a Member of Parliament in 1807 and died in Bath at Edgar Buildings in 1818.

One of the Franks at least was still regularly taking the mineral water treatments of pumping and bathing but the frequency had dropped to every two or three days. Nevertheless Old Norris and the pumper still got generous tips, 10/6d, for Old Norris and 7/- for the pumper.

Further health enhancing activities included horse rides in Sydney Gardens where 'an agreeable and much frequented ride' encircled the pleasure grounds.[119]

When the Franks left Bath on the 8th March the stay had cost £768 -19-10½d.

118   Fawcett, Trevor (2002) *Bath Commercialie'd*, Bath: Ruton, p. 84.

119   *Bath Chronicle*, 14/3/1799, p.1.

11

SEA WATER AND SODA WATER:
RAMSGATE AND MARGATE, SUMMER 1804

IN AUGUST 1804 the Franks arrived back at Ramsgate. They were without their butler John Freilick who had died earlier in the year at Isleworth. In his will[120] he made his fellow servant Sarah Liversedge, who had accompanied the Franks to Ramsgate, his executor and left her all his property including a 5% annuity. He also left two gold rings and £5 to William Edginton a fellow butler at a nearby country house. A new name appears in the accounts - Foulon the replacement butler - with small frequent payments to 'Foulon's book'. His first name Louis is revealed in Priscilla Franks' 1824 cash book[121] and he was almost certainly the Lewis Foulon who died in New Windsor in 1833.[122]

The party set out from Isleworth on the 2nd August, Jacob, Priscilla and Liversedge in the chaise and four, three maids were in another chaise and Foulon and Henry were in a barouche. They stayed overnight at the Fountain at Canterbury and arrived at Ramsgate on the 3rd August.[123] The household settled in a house rented for four weeks from Miss Elizabeth Veriar[124] for £29-8s.

The main purpose of the visit was sea water bathing which was undertaken on twelve occasions at a total cost of £2-8s and a 7/6d tip for the bathing attendant. However sea water was supported by a new taste for soda water, fizzy carbonated water that was bought eight times in Ramsgate,

120 National Archives, Will of John Frailick (Freilick), probate granted 12/4/1804, PROB 11/1407/111.

121 The full name is used in several places in the cash book that Priscilla used when a widow; one instance is the entry for 21/12/1824, London Metropolitan Archives, ACC/775/74.

122 Ancestry.co.uk

123 The Franks' travelling expenses cash book, London Metropolitan Archives, ACC/775/73.

124 Will of Elizabeth Veriar of Ramsgate, probate 5/4/1806, PROB 11/1442/30.

once in Margate and twice in Brighton as they made an excursion of their journey home. Joseph Priestley had discovered how to carbonate water in 1767 and John Nooth developed an efficient small scale carbonating process not long afterwards. At first soda water was treated as medicine. According to the then current MacBride Doctrine all organic bodies, including human bodies, were held together by 'mephitic air' [carbon dioxide] and when people had 'putrid diseases' or infections this binding gas was given off and inflammation resulted. So the treatment was to give the patient a good dose of carbon dioxide by drinking soda water to replace that lost because of the disease. The MacBride Doctrine was generally refuted by the 1780s but it was still widely agreed by the Bath physicians such as Dr Falconer that the carbon dioxide in Bath's mineral water had health benefits or, at the least, that the effervescence preserved other active ingredients of mineral water.[125] Consequently drinking carbonated water was considered very beneficial. The Bath controversialist Philip Thicknesse however mocked Falconer's belief that carbon dioxide was the active ingredient in the Bath mineral water.[126]

By the 1790s Johann Jacob Schweppes had developed a process to produce carbonated water at scale and to bottle it. The fact that the Franks bought their soda water on separate occasions, costing 7d each time, rather than buying a job lot of bottled water, suggests they were taking theirs at recently fashionable Soda Rooms where it was made and consumed immediately. The problem was the 'beneficial qualities of fixed [mephitic] air' could be lost from stone bottles by evaporation through bad corks or by keeping too long; so a Mr Burkitt invented a 'Sodaic Powder' that could be mixed in a tumbler of water to create healthy soda water.[127] Buying healthy water was accompanied by buying fruit including a pineapple, cost 2/-d, grapes and nectarines, and on the 23rd August 'various fruits' were eaten when they were at Margate. They had hampers of viands and vegetables shipped to them from London.

The stay in Ramsgate generally mirrored the Franks' trip there the previous year. They paid the subscription for Burgess's Rooms and library and paid to LeBas' [subscription] book at the Margate Assembly Rooms where he was still Master of Ceremonies. They paid two visits to the Dandelion pleasure ground, attended two balls and on the 11th August they paid 15/- for two tickets to Madame Bianchi's benefit concert at the Ramsgate Assembly Rooms.

125 Zuck, D. (1978) 'Dr Nooth and his Apparatus', *British Journal of Anaesthetics*, Vol, 50; 393, p398.

126 Thicknesse, Philip (n.d.) *An Epistle to Dr Wm. Falconer of Bath*, Bath: Pratt & Clinch.

127 *The Englishman* 3/8/187, p.1a.

Madame Bianchi was an up and coming soprano. She had been born Jane Jackson and married the famous Italian composer Francesco Bianchi. She had a long career and in 1818 she travelled to India and spent seven years there performing at the Court of the Nawab of Oudh. Joseph Farington the landscape painter and member of the Royal Academy was also at the Ramsgate concert and described it in his diary.[128]

> In the evening we went to Ramsgate to the Assembly Rooms where Madame Bianchi sang several songs to a piano forte and Meyer played at the harp. At ½ past nine the music was over. 7/6d was paid by each person for admittance. A ball then commenced. There was much company and among them Lady Augusta Murray and her son and her sister, Lady Hamilton with Mrs and Miss Nelson, Lord Essex and many officers of the Herefordshire Militia… Lord Cholmondeley was also there and also Lord Keith who commanded the Fleet in the Downs.

Mr Meyer was an accomplished harpist who had been born in Strasbourg. The company at the concert was rather louche. Lady Emma Hamilton was the mistress of Admiral Lord Nelson who at this time was at sea with the fleet. She was with Mrs Nelson the wife of Admiral Nelson's older brother Rev Dr William Nelson, a Prebendary of Canterbury Cathedral and was 'passing the summer' with them at their Prebendal House in Canterbury. Nelson's estranged wife meanwhile was said to be 'passing the summer in peaceful retirement and wholly secluded from the fashionable world'.[129] (By September however Lady Nelson had emerged into society by arriving at Bath).[130] Farington was unflattering about Lady Hamilton who had he thought 'grown prodigiously large and exposed her shoulders & breasts manifestly, having the appearance of one of the Bacchantes of Reuben'.

Augusta Murray another of the concert goers had clandestinely married the Duke of Sussex, the King's third son in Rome and although they had a further marriage ceremony in London the marriage was declared void under the Royal Marriages Act. By 1804 Augusta and the Duke were separated and

---

128 Farington, Joseph (n.d.) Ted. J. Greig *The Farington Diaries*, Vol.II, p.274-5. The presence of Lady Hamilton in Ramsgate is confirmed by a letter sent to her dated 29/9/1804 in which the correspondent apologised for not being able to meet her at Ramsgate. National Maritime Museum, Letters to Lady Hamilton, CRK/22/102.

129 *St James's Chronicle*, 4/8.1804, p.4.

130 *Bath Chronicle*, 3/9/1804, p.3d..

she was living in Ramsgate where she had listed herself as the Duchess of Sussex in the resort's directory. Lord Cholmondeley had been a well-known rake in his earlier days, allegedly having wagered Lord Derby that he could make love to a woman in a balloon 1,000 feet in the air. The presence of many officers may have been the reason why the Franks bought an Army List while in Ramsgate.

The Franks' visit to Ramsgate ended with a short tour on their way home to Isleworth. They sent two of their maids back to London by stage and they set off for Brighton with two other maids accompanying them. They stopped first at Dover on the 1st September, then passed through Romney and stayed at the George at Rye. From there they went on to Hastings where they stayed overnight at the Swan, then to Eastbourne where they had to 'lay' at the New Inn for 'want of horses'. When the horses were ready they moved on to Seaford and finally arrived at Brighton on the 4th September.[131] The next entry for the 5th September mentions 'play' at Brighton and there is a further mention of 'play 5/-d' on the 7th September. They stayed at the fashionable Castle Inn that was adjacent to the Prince Regent's summer pavilion (before it was transformed into an Indo-saracenic fantasy by Nash). The Castle had been rebuilt in 1766 when a new Assembly Rooms was added to it and decorated in the Adam style. The bill for the Castle was £29 plus £1 for the waiter, 10/-d for the maid, 2/6d for the 'boots' and 2/-d for the porter.

The Castle Inn at Brighton, to the left of the Brighton Pavilion: Yale Center for British Art, Paul Mellon Collection.

There is a cryptic entry for the 7th August that refers to 'Agamemnon 3/-d'. Most likely this was a visit to the navy frigate HMS Agamemnon but on the 6th August she was reported to be at Chatham, taking on guns and stores.[132]

131   The Franks' travelling expenses cash book, op cit.

132   *Kentish Gazette* 6/9/1804, *Commercial Chronicle*, 7/8/1804.

She had been decommissioned in 1792 but with the start of the Napoleonic Wars she was being refitted for service again. Had the ship sailed past Brighton on the way to be refitted and had the Franks hired a small boat to sail out to see her? The Agamemnon would have been an interesting ship to visit; Nelson had been its captain from 1793 to 1796 and it was reputedly his favourite vessel. It carried 64 guns and was at the Battle of Copenhagen in 1801 and the year after the Franks saw her she fought in the Battle of Trafalgar.

The party travelled home to Isleworth on the 10th September via Henfield and Horsham, dined at Dorking, and then continued through Epsom to home.

12
FAMILY CONNECTIONS:
BATH, WINTER SEASON, 1804-5

JACOB FRANKS BOUGHT a new wig, cost £1-16s, for the next visit to Bath in the 1804-5 winter season. They travelled along the Bath Road and 'lay, dined and breakfasted' at the White Hart at Marlborough. They bought two cheeses in the town before heading for Bath. They brought the usual retinue of servants with them; Foulon the butler, William Argent and Henry as footmen and Liversedge who was paid several times during the stay for 'house & washing'. There may have been a new housekeeper called Durand. As they arrived at Bath there was a payment of £25 entered in the cash book as 'Durand, house'. There followed a series of payments of £25, a penultimate one of £10 and then a final payment for the balance of Durand's account. Were these the costs of running the Franks' household during their stay in Bath or was it some other and mysterious payment?[133] The Franks also had three maids with them as they paid 'board wages' for three such on the 14th December. Foulon fell ill during the visit and the Franks bought him the patent medicine opedeldoc and paid for a session at the Hot Bath for him. Henry as a footman had the usual footman's perks of providing playing cards (which could be sold on after the master had finished with them).

As in previous visits to Bath the Franks frequently met with their relatives the Johnsons. Indeed the Johnsons had probably arranged their lodgings in the city with Mrs Molland of the confectionery shop. She owned No. 21 Milsom Street as well as the shop at No. 2.[134] Peter Nicholas Molland the original owner

133 There were ten payments to Durand during the visit totalling £210-15-7. Some of the entries had notation; 'paid Durand 24:lh bills', '11;lh ', and '7lh '. See 'Cryptics & Indecipherables' for an example entry. What the payments to Durand were for remains obscure.

134 No. 21 Milsom Street is identified as the house the Franks lodged in during their 1806 visit in a note on p. 3 of the cash book; that Mrs Molland was the landlord is confirmed in the cash book entries for that visit.

of Mollands had died in 1804 and his wife Dorothea, Mrs Molland, carried on the business very successfully becoming the main caterer for important social events such as the Harmonic Society concerts.[135] Soon after arriving in the city the Franks settled up with their brother-in-law General Johnson who had procured a supply of coal for them. Jacob bought or hired for £1-8s a secretaire, a writing desk, as well as the usual writing materials. These included wafer seals, a frequently purchased item that were used instead of wax to seal a letter. They were made from a mixture of flour, egg white, isinglass and yeast, dyed in various colours and baked to form wafers.[136] He also bought a Ready Reckoner, a small handbook of arithmetical tables for simplifying the calculation of the complex weights, measures and currency units used at that time.

The Franks had hosted the General's two sons in Ramsgate the previous year. General Sir Henry Johnson[137] had married Jacob Franks' sister Rebecca Franks in New York in 1782. Theirs was an unlikely connection. Rebecca was always known as Becky and grew up in Philadelphia and by the age of nineteen was well-educated, confident and considered a great beauty.[138] She was sociable and flirtatious and enjoyed the social whirl of Philadelphia as one of its young 'beaux'. In a letter in 1784 remembering these times she wrote to a friend 'if you see B. Tilghman tell him his old flirt sends him her love'.[139] In the fall of 1777 during the War of Independence the British army was quartered in Philadelphia and the presence of so many officers added to the social gaiety of the city. Becky was one of the young women who attended the grand ball that was given the comically fictitious name of a Mischianza. Becky and Henry Johnson probably first met at the ball. Becky had a wonderful time that evening but it linked her and her family with the British and the American Tory loyalists of the city who were much resented by the city's radicals. The consequence was that when the British army left Philadelphia the independence minded Radicals put enough pressure on David Franks and his family to force them to remove to New York. Becky continued with her

135   *Bath Chronicle*, 12/4/1804, p.3c., 1/2/1810, p.3b., Dorothea died in 1813.

136   'Lady Smatter' (2015) 'Sealing with wafer seals', Her reputation for accomplishment: records of skills and pastimes of the Jane Austen Era (1770-1820), Blog, Her reputation for accomplishment. WordPress.

137   Portrait of Henry Johnson, National Portrait Gallery, ref. NPGD36545.

138   The Susser Archive; JCR-UK, History of the Great Synagogue, Chp. 5, 'Moses Hart's School, 1722, https://www.jewishgen.org.uk/susser/roth/chfive.htm.

139   Stern, Mark Abbott (n.d.) Dear Mrs Cad: a Revolutionary war letter of Rebecca Franks, https://sites/americanjewisharchives.org/publications.

amusements as a young attractive woman in New York even though by then she had become engaged to Henry Johnson and they married on the 24th January 1782. The gossips said that 'he who was willing to run the gauntlet of Miss Franks' daring raillery must have been a brave man'.[140] Soon after the wedding they travelled to England and settled in Bath.

Colonel Sir Henry Johnson c.1801: courtesy of the Look & Learn Historical Picture Library

Henry Johnson was Irish, born in Kilteran, Co. Dublin in 1748.[141] He became an officer in the British army and when serving in America during the War of Independence he was twice captured by the American rebels. After his marriage to Becky the couple returned to live in Bath but in 1784 they were living at Killarney Castle in Ireland. Becky was uncomfortable in the 'old and musty castle' and she grew nostalgic for Philadelphia. She wrote in 1784 to her friend of Philadelphia days 'Mrs Cad' in America, the wife of General Cadwallader, that she was 'nostalgic to visit Philadelphia again but can never hope of it… whilst he [Henry Johnson] can he will stay, either in Ireland (where we are now) or *England and as his wife I* must obey.[142] However they did not remain in Ireland or England as Johnson was sent to Nova Scotia to command the 17th Regiment of Foot. Their son Henry Allen Johnson was born in Nova Scotia in 1785. In 1787 the regiment returned to Britain and their second son George Pigot Johnson was baptised in Chatham, probably soon after the regiment's return.

It is not known where Becky and Henry settled on their return but from 1793 Henry Johnson was again serving in Ireland. There he was an advocate of harsh measures against the United Irishmen in Ulster. He played a major role in suppressing the Wexford rebellion and on 5th June 1798 he repulsed a rebel

140   Stern, Mark Abbott(n.d.) op cit.; also reprinted in Stern (2010) op cit. p.162.

141   Chichester, H. M. revised by Blackstock, A. F. (2004) 'Johnson, Sir Henry, first baronet, (1748-1835)', *Oxford Dictionary of National Biography*, Oxford: Oxford University Press, available online, https://doi.org/10.1093/ref:odnd/14886.

142   Stern, Mark Abbott (n.d.) 'Dear Mrs Cad: a Revolutionary War Letter of Rebecca Franks', op cit.

force of between 10 and 15 thousand men with an irregular force of 1,400 troops. His losses were 90 men the rebels lost about 1,500. Johnson had two horses shot from under him during the action. He was lionised as 'the saviour of the south' of Ireland for Britain.

The *Bath Journal* noted the arrival of General and Mrs Johnson in the city on the 10th October 1803.[143] Later when Henry Johnson was retired the couple lived in Bath at Catherine Place in a house owned by Priscilla Franks and in 1818 Henry Johnson was made baronet of Bath.

The Franks were closely involved with the Johnsons during their stay. They were particularly generous with their nephews George and Henry Johnson. They were both given £5 on Christmas Day and later they bought the two young men new pairs of breeches, a pair was also bought for their cousin William Cooper. The brothers were given another ten guineas at the end of January. Mrs Johnson was given £35 in February. The Johnson's servants were employed on occasion by the Franks who gave the coachman a tip of 1/-d and the servant 2/-d. The Franks' relative Andrew Hamilton, who had been with them in Bath in earlier visits, was also probably living in city at this time and there was a small payment to a 'AH' early in the visit.

Jacob and Priscilla also had more distant relations in Bath.[144] Jacob's aunt Phila Franks (1722-1811) had married Oliver De Lancey in New York in 1742; their daughter Susanna De Lancey became the second wife of Sir William Draper when the couple married in New York in 1770. William Draper had served in the army in India and had led an expedition to take Manilla in 1762. In his retirement he lived in Bath and Clifton and in the later 1760s he was subject to attacks in the newspapers by the anonymous critic Junius, who was actually Philip Francis the son of one of Draper's friends in Bath.[145] Probably to escape the furore he toured America; where he married Susanna. They had two daughters, Phila Augusta and Anna Susanna and the family lived at Clifton. When Susanna died in 1774 the two girls lived with Draper's cousin

143   *Bath Journal* 24/10/1803, p.3c..

144   Parkes, Joseph, & Merrivel, H. (1867) *Memoirs of Sir Philip Francis with Correspondence and Journals,* London: Longman. Vol. I. pp, 224-226. Ancestry. co.uk. Gore Douglas, (2017) *The Scandalous Family of Mrs Anne Collins, widow, of Ashley Grove,* available on the World Wide Web at URL: http://www. boxpeopleandplaces.co.uk/mrs-ann-collins.html

145   Junius was one of several pseudonyms used by Philip Francis when he conducted a press campaign between 1769 and 1772 lampooning and criticising the government and particular individuals such as William Draper. Francis was a frequent visitor to Bath at that time where he 'lived as a raike'.

Anne Collins and her naval officer husband at Bladud Buildings in Bath. Sir William Draper was buried at St Swithin's and there is a memorial to him in Bath Abbey. Phila died in 1782 and later Anna Susanna, whose married name was Gore, became very wealthy when she inherited £10,000 from 'a relative' – possibly from one of the extended Franks/De Lancey family?

Jacob Franks having had cousins living at Bath illustrates how the city was at the centre of an intricate network of family and social relations that stretched between the British upper classes and across the British colonies. The social context of Bath enabled connections to be made across the tiers of social hierarchy. When Jacob's cousin Anna Susanna Gore, of American parentage, died very young as a widow at Hotwells in 1793 she made bequests in her will to the Countess of Bessborough of a mahogany tea chest with silver canisters, and a picture and a pair of gloves to the Countess' daughter Lady Caroline Ponsonby, better known as Lady Caroline Lamb. Anna Gore, the Countess and her daughter had probably all mingled together and become friends at Bath. Both mother and daughter acquired an air of notoriety[146] which perhaps made them more socially accessible to the De Lancey sisters.

The Franks, to further explore Bath as a social nexus, were linked with both parties to the Draper/Junius controversy through a matrix of family and colonial connections.[147] Rebecca Johnson, Jacob's sister, had a childhood friend and 'old flirt' from Philadelphia, mentioned earlier, called B. Tilghman. He was William 'Bill' Tilghman (b.1756) and he had an older brother Richard Tilghman born in Maryland in 1746. Richard was sent to England for his legal training and there he became friends with his relative Philip Francis who as

146   Countess Bessborough was married to an abusive husband and had several affairs including one with Richard Brinsley Sheridan. Lady Caroline Lamb became famous as the lover of Lord Byron.

147   Identification of Bill Tilghman, Stern op cit. p. 205 & p. 239 note 38: the Tilghman family tree, catalogue entry for Tilghman family papers, Maryland Center for History and Culture & Verity, B. (2016) 'Edward III Descents for Lt Philemon Tilghman (1760-1797)' Royal Descent; Blog 9/5/2016,: Richard Tilghman leaves America for India, Bryan, J. A. "The Horrors of Civil War" The Tilghman family in the American Revolution', *Maryland Historical Journal*, p. 34. Visits to Bath, Parkes, Joseph, & Merrivel, H. op cit. pp. 242-3, 270-1; Chabot, Charles & Twistleton, Edward (1871) *The Handwriting of Junius*, London: John Murray, p.238: Miss Giles verses, Wharton, Anne Hollingsworth (1893) *Through Colonial Doors*, Philadelphia: Lippincott. The American land purchases, Francis, Beata & Keary Eliza (n.d) *The Francis Letters by Sir Philip Francis (with a note on the Junius Controversy by C. F. Keary)*, London: Hutchinson Vol. 1, pp. 108-123: Richard Tilghman was the son of Turbutt Francis's sister, op cit. p.124.

Junius was then conducting his newspaper campaign against Draper, against other particular individuals, and against the government generally. In May 1770 the pair made a horseback tour of Wiltshire and ended their trip at Bath. At Christmas that year they were both together again in Bath where they enjoyed every species of '*debauché*'. Francis, whose wife remained in London, became infatuated with a Miss Giles at Bath and danced with her all evening at one ball in the Lower Assembly Rooms. He then addressed amatory verses to her which Tilghman copied out and delivered to the lady. (These verse later became evidence in the long running argument over the identity of Junius). By the end of 1771 Tilghman had returned to Philadelphia and when Francis complained that his Christmas 1771 visit to Bath was dull Tilghman replied 'I am sorry you found Bath dull, at the same time I feel a sort of pride in thinking the want of my company was, in some measure, the occasion of it being less agreeable to you'. Philip Francis used Richard and a mutual American cousin called Turbutt Francis to help him purchase 1,000 acres of land in Indian Territory in America, west of the Ohio River. But Francis's career was not to be in America but in India and in 1774 he sailed to Calcutta as one of the four members of the new Governing Council of Bengal. Richard Tilghman left Philadelphia in 1777, (at about the time that Rebecca Franks as she then was and probably Bill Tilghman, were enjoying the Mischianza ball in Philadelphia) and became a lawyer for the East India Company in Calcutta . His family nickname was 'East India Dick' and he died at sea in 1786 while sailing back from Calcutta. By then Rebecca was living in Bath and may well have met Philip Francis who was visiting Bath in the winter of 1789-1790 and probably visited the city on other occasions. The Franks, the Tilghman, the De Lancey, the Draper and the Francis families were enmeshed with each other, with and through, the city of Bath.

Returning to the Franks' daily life in Bath one new feature in the cash book for this visit was a series of entries of payments to 'Mrs F' totalling £45 suggesting that Priscilla was spending money according to her own wishes that did not find an entry in the cash book.

The Franks did not immediately renew their subscriptions to the Assembly Rooms but did renew the subscription to the Club at York House (£15-15-6d). They attended a dinner at the club on the 8th January that cost £1-11-6d. Jacob was also playing cards at the club and according to an entry on the 1st March 'lost at the Club £21-1s.'; perhaps that is why to improve his play he bought a copy of 'Hints at Whist'.[148] Jacob Franks may also have been losing money at cards at home rather than at the club, there is an entry for the 16th January 'lost 1 guinea at home'.

148   Haslam. P. (1790) '*Hints to Whist Players for the Use of Private Parties*'.

THE CLUB IN THE 1800s

In his satire of Bath life 'Bath Characters'[149] published in 1807 Richard Warner talks about 'the CLUB' as primarily a place for gambling. He was probably referring to the Bath Club. In this extract 'Ramrod' (James King Master of the Ceremonies of the Upper Rooms) is conversing with 'Tom Rattle' (Major Matthews) who has just returned to Bath after several years away.

Ram: What improvements do you find have taken place amongst us during your absence – the CLUB –

> *Rat*: Oh! Name it not for pity's sake – nothing but long faces and empty pockets – "a waste and a howling wilderness", naked as eastern Prussia and *drained* as dry as Holland, Every rook pigeoned and every knowing one taken in. Lord *Patterboard* has just paid his *friends* there a visit, and introduced a new jerk of the elbow of his own invention; thrown a *six ace* nine times running, swept the table with the rapidity of one of Buonaparte's marches; and set off again for London in his post-chaise and four, carrying away in his pocket every *rouleau* the house could muster.

Card playing was more prominent in the Franks' domestic social life. They again hosted a rout to play cards at their lodgings in January, with the catering by Molland's and the extra tables and chairs hired from Bally the Milsom Street auctioneer. The party may have become boisterous as the Franks had to pay Mrs Molland £2-18-6d for broken crockery when they settled up their lodging bill. Jacob may even have placed a ½ guinea bet on a race horse called Fair Play on New Year's Eve but the entry is too cryptic to be certain.[150]

Taking the mineral water cures was still an important part of the stay. There are 21 entries paying for dry pumping and for bathing chairs to and from the Baths; sometimes receiving 400 strokes of the pump costing 2/- but mostly 200 strokes. On the 26th February Franks gave Old Norris the Guide at the Baths 10/6d and the pumper 7/-. There were another six entries for bathing and also three for 'bath tubs' at a cost of 1/-d per occasion, these may

149   Warner, Richard, op cit, p. 5.

150   Fair Play was a name used for horses, Tattersalls were selling a black gelding called Fair Play in 1802. *Morning Post* 29/5/1802

have been an alternative to bathing in one of the three hot springs. Sometimes as on the 18th January a visit to the Baths was accompanied by a visit to the alehouse and often by the purchase of barley drops. At the end of the stay in the city the Franks paid the bills of Garthwaite the druggist and Phillott the surgeon, who had probably bled Franks as part of the treatment.

At the start of the Bath season in October Mr Stroud, the tenant manager of the Upper Assembly Rooms, and Mr Tyson the Master of Ceremonies announced an increase in the cost of subscriptions to the balls 'flattering [themselves] a small advance in the subscription to the balls will not be deemed unreasonable'.[151] Dress Balls were to be held on Mondays and a subscription to all 28 was 12/-, 24s bought 2 tickets for the balls with the ladies ticket being transferable between women of the family. The Cotillion or Fancy Balls were to be held on Thursday and the subscription for all 28 was the same as for the Dress Balls but 6d had to be paid on admission for tea. The Franks bought both subscriptions for £2-4s each [24/-d]. They attended at least two of the Dress Balls as well as the Masters of Ceremonies Benefit Balls, Tyson's at the Upper Rooms on the 7th January and King's at the Lower Rooms on the 11th. They went to five Cotillion Balls at the Upper Rooms and duly paid the sixpences for their tea.

Music was still important. They did not buy a whole subscription to Mr Rauzzini's concerts at the Upper Rooms but they did attend the eighth, tenth, eleventh and twelfth of the series paying the 6/- entrance for non-subscribers. The twelfth concert featured in the first act a piano forte concerto by Mr Griffin and a violin concerto by Mr Binger followed in the second act by works by Haydn and Handel with a 'full band and orchestra'. The Franks were at the Second Harmonic Society's Ladies' Nights at the Lower Rooms on the 4th January. General Johnson of course was one of the Stewards and organisers of the event[152] and was much involved in organising the Harmonic Society's balls and concerts from 1804 to at least 1818. This perhaps meant that his wife Becky who had missed the pleasures of balls and parties after leaving Philadelphia could once again enjoy such events. In April 1804 before the Franks had arrived at Bath General Johnson was the president of the Society when it held a grand Fete Champetre at Sydney Gardens[153] and although we do not know if Becky attended it seems likely that as the president's wife would have been there.

151   *Bath Journal* 8/10/1804. P.3c..

152   *Bath Journal* 28/1/1805, p. 3d.

153   *Bath Journal*, 23/4/1804, p.3d.

Stewarding the Harmonic Society's events at Sydney Gardens was sometimes contentious. The 'White Hart Harmonic Society' Gala held there on 21st May 1805 was crowded with a thousand people, 700 of whom were 'ladies beautifully dressed'.

The weather was lovely – and all went on charmingly till the Ices and Jellies were to be distributed. And then such a confusion and scramble, I never saw – waiters running to particular Boxes – Gentlemen, nay Ladies too –snatching as they passed, Tis not to be described but the worst of all a serious discord happened [ ]. The Revd Mr Bowen [ ] one of the principals of the Society – was accosted by Sir George Colebrooke, and charged with being inattentive in his office. Mr Bowen, being from Wales – look you went into a passion, and spoke hot words, when Sir George thinking to cool him threw a Glass of Ice in his face.[154]

Fists were raised and sticks shaken. John Bowen was the founder of the Harmonic Society, well known to be pugnacious and was satirised by Warner in the 'Bath Characters' as 'Mr Bow-wow'. George Colebrooke was an acquaintance and business associate of the Franks.

The other usual amusements continued during the Franks' stay; treats at Molland's - orangeade on the 16th February - riding their horses around the Sydney Gardens ride as well as visiting the gardens themselves. Jacob Franks may have gone for country walks, he bought a 'pair of mud boots' for 16/- in December. There were visits to the theatre. On Saturday 9th February Jacob and Priscilla saw 'John Ball or the Englishman's Fire Side' followed by a farce called 'Raising the Wind'. They bought tickets for their servant Henry to go to the theatre the following day and a ticket for Foulon on the 21st. The Franks were probably having a portrait painted as they paid the 'portrait painter' 5 guineas.

Food and drink feature in the cash book. They bought wine from Mr Stroud who was a wine merchant as well the manager of the Upper Rooms and bought a dozen wine glasses. At the end of January they had two bottles of champagne and they still enjoyed the cheeses they bought from Minifee's in Cheap Street. Many of the entries for food were for items they bought to send to friends and relatives, as was usually the case when they were in Bath. Cream and cheese from Minifee were sent to the regular recipients Mrs Spilsbury and Mr Vanderheyden. Other cheeses were sent to a Mr Hodges and 'Duncan'.

154 Burnim, Kalman A. *The Letters of Sarabond William Siddons to Hester Lynch Piozzi in the John Ryland's Library* footnote p.79.

Lady Isabella Cooper was firstly sent cheese and later she was sent lamb and then mutton to her house at Thurlow. Jacob, Priscilla and 'AH' (Andrew Hamilton) had visited her at Thurlow the previous autumn after returning to Isleworth from Ramsgate and before moving onto Bath.[155]

The Franks generally kept abreast of affairs back in Isleworth. At the end of December they paid £2 towards 'John Wilkinson of Isleworth's petition' posted to Mrs Spilsbury. John Wilkinson was a Lincoln's Inn lawyer whose family lived at Isleworth but what the petition concerned is unknown. Another obscure and difficult to read entry for the 20th February 1805 is: 'Subscrd: to Marquis St Leger 5-/-'.[156] This is unlikely to have been a bet or subscription on a horse called Marquis at the St Leger sweepstake horse race at Doncaster because this did not take place until September. There was a French Marquis de St Leger dancing a cotillion at the ball during the Romney races in August that year;[157] but if that was the Marquis of Franks' cash book why did he need a subscription?

The waiters at the Upper Rooms received their usual Christmas box of 15/6d and the Franks also donated to a subscription fund for 'George the waiter', probably a waiter at the Rooms who had fallen on hard times. A 'poor woman' was given 5/-d. and they paid £1 as recompense to the ostler who had been kicked by their horse.

At the end of February 1805 they prepared to leave Bath, they paid for the newspapers, they settled with Mitchell the tailor, and Flook the boot maker, they had some trunks made or repaired and the coach was made ready at the coach makers. They bought 3 barrels of oysters – were they to take back with them to Isleworth? Jacob and Priscilla travelled home in their chaise and four [horses], Foulon, Liversedge and a kitchen maid travelled in a chaise and pair, four other servants (probably William, Henry and two maids) were in a coach and four. The groom and his helper had set out the day before the others with three saddle horses.[158]

---

155   Franks travel expenses book op cit.

156   It is possible this is a mis-reading, the original entry can be seen in appendix 3.

157   *Morning Herald*, 31/8/1805.

158   The Franks travel expenses account book, entry for 1/3/1805, London Metropolitan Archives, ACC/775/73.

13

Consulting the Doctor:
Bath & Clifton, May 1806

Jacob Franks made a brief visit to Bath arriving on the 15th May 1806 without Priscilla, (only the arrival of a Mr Franks is reported in the newspaper arrivals sections) but he was accompanied by his servants Foulon and George. He travelled via Salisbury and on arrival he stayed overnight at the White Hart before moving into lodgings at No. 21 Milsom Street, at 3 guineas for two weeks, rented from Mrs Molland. While in Bath Franks renewed his subscription to the Club but not that to the Assembly Rooms. The visit was primarily for medical reasons. He consulted Dr Gibbes, who had been the Franks' Bath physician since at least 1803, on the 16th, 17th, 18th, 21st and 22nd of May for a fee of a guinea each occasion. No doubt on Gibbes' advice he went to the Baths on the 16th May and had a bath tub at the cost of a shilling on the 22nd. On the 21st a 'man for leeching' came to bleed Franks and the following day Phillott the surgeon came for cupping. This method could be used to treat sciatica and muscle pain; a heated glass vessel was placed over the skin creating a vacuum, as it cooled it drew the skin into the vessel. Gibbes was satirised by Richard Warner in 'Bath Characters'[159] as Dr Faddle who told 'Signora Ratanna' a leading socialite of the Rooms, 'never distress yourself my dear Madame; a purge and a blister, a bleeding and a clyster will set all right again'. He was however prescribing for the Signora's pet dog. It seems that Franks avoided the purge, blister and the clyster. However eating oranges may also have been part of Gibbes' prescription, Franks bought them every two days during his stay.

On the 23rd Franks went to stay at Clifton, Bristol probably travelling in a coach borrowed from General Johnson. In 1806 the spa at Hotwells at the foot of the river cliff below Clifton village was in decline but the village above it had been developed with fine Georgian terraces although the start of the Napoleonic Wars had brought a temporary suspension to the suburb's

159 Warner, Richard, (1808) *Bath Characters*, 2nd. ed. p. 17.

Avon Gorge and Clifton in early nineteenth century: courtesy of Akeman Press.

expansion. Franks stayed in Clifton until the 26th May and his hotel bill, in addition to the tips for the waiters, maid and boots, included a guinea for what seems to read, improbably, as 'airing toll'. Clifton with its location above the Avon Gorge was known for the purity of its air and a ride on the Downs was regarded as restorative of health so perhaps Gibbes had sent Franks there to take the air as part of his cure and the 'toll' was for some kind of fresh air therapy such as riding or walking on private paths, or perhaps the entry does not read as airing toll at all?

Back in Bath on the 28th May Franks paid Molland's bill for his lodgings, paid the bills of Garthwayt the druggist and Sheid the grocer, gave General Johnson's coachman and footman a tip and of course bought cheeses from Minifee. Then he returned home to Isleworth, taking with him some flannel he had bought to make a pelisse for Priscilla and some shirts for himself. The cost of the visit was £80-10-0½d.; the board wages for George the servant were £2-5s and £2-2s for Foulon.

14

CONFECTIONERY AND SWEETS:
BATH, SPRING SEASON, 1807

THE FRANKS ARRIVED at Bath for their seventh visit on the 10th March and had dinner at the White Hart in Bath. Foulon the butler, Liversedge and Anthony/Antonio Gorla had arrived with them. Gorla had been employed by them as a servant at least as early as 1805 probably as a cook or a confectioner and he had accompanied Jacob on visits to West Harling in 1805. A couple of days later their goods from London arrived on Lye's waggon; George Lye was a Bath carrier, with his 'compting house' in Broad Street, who ran regular waggons between Bath and London. He had bought the business from John Wiltshire in 1800[160] to add to his existing carrier business between Bath, Warminster and Salisbury. Wiltshire's 'Flying Waggons' that made the journey between Bath and London in two and a half days had been established by John Wiltshire's great uncle and developed into a prosperous business by his father Walter who had become very wealthy, a friend of Thomas Gainsborough the painter and who built a grand Palladian mansion at Shockerwick near Bath.

Jacob and Priscilla were settled for a comfortable stay. This would include a substantial sum spent on wine, pastries, confectionaries and visits to Molland's the confectioners in Milson Street. The Franks also bought in a supply of expensive 'Sp[ermaceti]: Candles' that were made from whale oil.

The Franks expenditure on wine & confectionery

14th March	Orangeade & jelley	2/-	17th April	Mollands	2/2
18th March	Decanter corks ½ doz	1/6	20th April	Mollands	1/2
ditto	Almon^d [almond] paste	3/6	22nd April	Mollands	1/4

160   *The Times*, 14/4/1800, p.2.

23rd March	Soda	-/ 8	24th April	Mollands	1/-	
6th April	Orangeade	1/-	25th April	Mollands	-/6	
7th April	Jelleys	2/-	27th April	Mollands	1/-	
9th April	Jelley 2/- Mada bunns 4d	2/4	29th April	Mollands	1/-	
10th April	jelly & buns	2/6	30th April	Mollands	1/2	
11th April	jelly & buns	2/6	ditto	Clarke the brewer	£8-8-6	
13th April	lemonade	1/6	1st May	Mollands	1/2	
14th April	Mada buns	-/4	2nd May	Mada [wine] 7/- Champge [champagne] £1-4s from Stroud	£1-4s.	
15th April	Orangeade					
		1/2				
			4th May	Mollands	1/-	

There is an entry for 'the club 1/6d' which was probably for refreshments at the Club. The entry for 'Mada buns' refers to Royal Madeira buns that in Bath were 'made and sold only by J Bedford'. They were probably intended to accompany Madeira wine, which we see the Franks also bought. These provided an alternative to the ordinary buns that are mentioned, several varieties of which were available. There were Bath buns made from sweetened milk based yeast dough, Sally Lunn buns, a type of brioche bun and Bath Wigs, a breakfast bun served in wedge shapes and flavoured with caraway seeds. Up to Easter 1807 Bedford's shop was in Union Passage but by November that year it had moved to the more salubrious and fashionable Bath Street (where the Bath Thermae is now). There was also a restaurant on the premises serving snack dishes.[161]

While they were in Bath the Franks were also paying in instalments a large bill of £122 to Antonio Gorla. As the cash book uses the term 'house' as code for their household expenses and as the references are to 'Gorla/house' perhaps they were entertaining lavishly and Gorla was providing the refreshments and confectionery? Gorla did well enough to be able a few years later to open a bakery and shop in Richmond not far from Isleworth advertising himself as French & Italian pastry cook and confectioner.[162] The Franks also

161 *Bath Journal*, 30/11/1807, p.2b.. Madeira buns were also sold in Leamington Spa in 1829, *Leamington Spa Courier*, 4/7/1829, p.2.

162 The shop was at George Street, Richmond. Anthony/Antoni, Gorla, born near

J. BEDFORD,
CONFECTIONER and COOK,
(Formerly of BOND-STREET, late of UNION-PASSAGE,)
Respectfully informs the Nobility, Gentry, and the Public, that he is removed to the
CORNER of NEW BATH-STREET,
Opposite to St. JAMES's-PARADE, near the HOT-BATH PUMP-ROOM; where he humbly solicits their kind patronage and support, assuring them it shall be his constant study to deserve it.
A ROOM for REFRESHMENTS; where is always ready to be Served-up BRITISH TURTLE SOUPS, PETIT OYSTER PIES and PATTIES, &c. &c.
All Sorts of PICKLES and PRESERVES, ESSENCE of ANCHOVIES, MUSHROOM-CATSUP, &c.
ROYAL MADEIRA BUNS, (made and sold only by J. BEDFORD,) carefully packed and sent to any part of the kingdom.
☞ A DRAWING-ROOM and other APART-MENTS, Genteely Furnished, to LET by the Month or Year.

Madeira Buns: courtesy of Bath Record Office.

hosted a rout while they were in Bath and on this occasion the catering was by Molland's and cost them £3-2-6d, Bally the auctioneer of Milsom Street again provided the chairs.

Whether Dr Gibbes thought their consumption of sugar a good thing is not known but they did pay him a guinea for a consultation. This was followed by the usual mineral water regime. Seventeen sessions of pumping, a session every day and three sessions of bathing. Two boxes of unspecified pills were purchased from Garthwayt the druggist. The bottles of Warner's Milk of Roses, a patent skin cream and Gattie's Esprit de Rose,[163] a perfume or eau de toilette, were probably for Priscilla.

When they had arrived in Bath the Franks had paid a guinea to each of the Masters of Ceremonies, by this time two new ones were installed, Charles LeBas, whom the Franks knew from Margate, was at the Lower Room replacing James King who had moved to the Upper Rooms. After that there is no further mention of the Rooms or balls but plays did frequently figure in the cash book. These entries definitely refer to the theatre rather than card playing because two are for '2 tickets for the play 10/-d' though most 'play' entries are just for a single ticket; it is not known whether the more avid playgoer was Jacob or Priscilla. One of the entries for the 14th April names the play and reads 'play (Jane Shore) 5/-d'.[164] This is the 1714 historical tragedy written by Nicholas Rowe about Jane Shore the mistress of Edward

Milan, died in 1810 and his stock-in-trade and equipment were put up for auction. Items included preserves, jellies, syrups, ices and wine, stoves, paste warmers, ice moulds and freezing pales. The shop was probably quite grand because also included were a counter, glass cases tiles, a shew board, shew glasses and a bow window complete'. In his will he was most concerned that his business should survive him. *Morning Advertiser* 19/10/1812 p. 4.

163 The cash book just states Milk of Rose and Esprit de Rose but newspaper advertisements identify them as patent products.

164 *Bath Chronicle*, 6/4/1807, p.3e, 13/4/1807, p. 3d.

IV and the leading role was played by the famous actress Mrs Sarah Siddons. She had first appeared in the Bath theatre in 1778 and by 1807 she was coming to the end of her long career. She finally retired in 1812, but in 1807 she was still a great Box Office draw. Mrs Siddons was doing a season at the Theatre Royal in the city and both of the Franks also went to see her in 'The Gamester' on the 4th April and one of them also saw her as Zara in 'The Mourning Bride'. During the season Siddons had also performed in 'Pizarro', which the Franks had seen during a much earlier visit to Bath, in 'Macbeth', that was probably Siddons' most famous role, and also 'George Barnwell', a popular play by George Lillo written in 1731 in which Siddons played Millwood a 'lady of pleasure'. Her last performance on the 11th April was as Queen Catherine in 'Henry VIII'.

Mrs Sarah Siddons as Jane Shore 1791: courtesy of the Look & Learn Historical Picture Library.

These theatre outings would have been much more comfortable than those on previous visits because they took place in the new Theatre Royal. The old one in Orchard Street put on its last performance on the 13th July 1805 and the first performance in the new theatre in Sawclose was on the 12th of October in that year. Coaches were asked to deliver and pick up patrons from Sawclose but the Franks were sedan chair users and they entered and exited through the grand entrance front facing Beauford Square. Only one concert is mentioned in the cash book and that was by Madame Angelica Catalani an Italian singer who had risen to great fame and celebrity performing in Paris, Venice and Lisbon and who had recently come to perform in Britain. She was said to have a full, powerful and clear voice performing a repertoire of oratorios by Handel and Haydn as well as Italian opera.

These activities kept Jacob and Priscilla amused in March and April 1807 but there were occasional new pastimes; on the 28th April they went to view an exhibition of gems, something that Priscilla with her family's background as diamond merchants may have found particularly engaging. Mr Findley who

New Theatre Royal, 1818: courtesy of Akeman Press.

ran a 'cabinet of gems' on Chapel Row near Queen Square was retiring and was selling his stock at reduced prices, he also put on display for a shilling a ticket 'the celebrated singing bird of Switzerland and the Chinese Mouse wrought in a fine enamelled gold and oriental pearls'.[165] A tour of Prior Park on the hills overlooking the city from the south cost 3/-; in 1807 the property still belonged to descendants of Ralph Allen but the following year it would be sold out of the family.

Prior Park: author's collection.

There are two entries in the cash book for 'Fair Play', the meaning is unknown but it was speculated earlier that it might be the name of a race horse? The servants were allowed some entertainment. William was given a shilling to see the 'Wild Beasts'. This was Mr Polito's 'Living Curiosities'[166] show that

165   *Bath Chronicle* 4/5/1807.

166   *Bath Journal* 23/3/1807, p2d, , *Bath Chronicle* 26/3/1807, p.3d.

The advertisement for Polito's menagerie: courtesy of Bath Record Office.

had set up in a yard off Walcot Street. The animals including a lion, tiger and kangaroo were exhibited in six 'large and commodious caravans' that were linked together to make a living diorama of the 'wonderful productions of nature'. As well as William the Franks had brought their other servants, Foulon, Henry, George and Sarah Liversedge, now working as house keeper, with them.

On the 4th May the Franks settled all their bills, Mrs Bourke was paid for their accommodation and an extra sum for having the furniture washed. This was probably the Miss Elizabeth Bourke who died aged 62 in 1812 at No. 24 Brock Street, Bath and so it is possible this was where the Franks had been lodging. Old Norris and the pumper received their usual tips. Mr Abbott Dore the hatter and hosier of No. 8 Abbey Churchyard who had earlier been paid the substantial sum of £7-16s on 20th March was paid an additional £2-15-6d on the 1st May. Jacob and Priscilla had kept in touch with Henry and Rebecca Johnson during their stay, the Johnsons had again organised their coal deliveries for them, and on Easter Day they had given Rebecca £20. The Franks' coach had been in Fullers coachworks for repairs during the stay but before they left Bath the coach needed further emergency repairs to the spring and wheels; then they left for Isleworth. The total cost of this last fully recorded visit by the Franks was £489 -4s -11d, or a daily cost of £8 -17s - 10¼d. The daily cost of their first recorded visit in 1777 was £4 -8s - 10¼d and so inflation had doubled the cost of a visit to Bath over three decades.

15

THE FINAL STAY:
BATH, SPRING SEASON, 1808

T HE FINAL VISIT recorded in the cash book was between the 4th March and the 25th April 1808 and it largely replicated the pattern of the previous year's stay. They paid Mrs Molland for coal, beef and mutton and so were presumably again staying at her lodging house. They paid Mrs Becky Johnson £25. The subscription to the York House Club was renewed and they paid a guinea to each of the Masters of Ceremonies, still Mr King and Mr LeBas. (Though the latter would be ousted in 1810 in a coup by subscribers who objected to him also remaining Master of Ceremonies at Margate).[167] A rigorous regime of taking the mineral water cure was undertaken; 20 pumping sessions and 5 bathing sessions. Old Norris was still about and received his usual tip as did the pumper who on this occasion was named as Mr Lyon. The therapeutic regime was balanced by visits to Molland's for refreshments, this establishment accounted for 23 visits, and the club, 2 visits. As on earlier stays there were plenty of entries for eatables including the inevitable cheeses from Minifee, lots of barley sugar, buns, oranges and spruce beer, this was a brew introduced from America that was made with the buds and tips of the spruce tree and molasses. It was very popular in Regency times and even Jane Austen was known to have brewed it at home. Over two dozen bottles of soda water, probably carbonated Bath mineral water, were bought.

Madame Catalani, who had performed in Bath the previous year, gave two grand subscription concerts in the city under the direction of Mr Rauzzini. The Franks attended the one on the 9th March. The concert was not a great success. Mrs Lybbe Powis who was also at the event described in her diary[168] how a thousand people had arrived at the Assembly Rooms very early to get

167   *Bath Chronicle*, 8/11/1810, 25/10/1810, Anon (1811) *The Wonders of a Week in Bath: in a doggerel verse address to the Hon T.S_____ , from T_____ Esq.*, pp.38-42.

168   Marks, Stephen Powys (2002) 'The Journals of Mrs Philip Lybbe Powys (1738-1817) A Half Century of Visits to Bath', *Bath History* vol.IX, pp. 58-59.

Madame Catalani in the role of Semiramis, 1818: courtesy of the Look & Learn Historical Picture Library

a good seat but when the concert was due to begin Rauzzini announced that Madame Catalani was suffering from a violent cold and sore throat and was too ill to sing the songs programmed but she would sing some others; 'we began to fear a riot as some hisses began, however, Madame came, and I dare say did what she was able'. She sang three songs and a duet with Signor Righi the 1st tenor of the London Opera House[169] but then 'was quite unable to Sing & retired with numbers of apologies'. Extra concerts were announced to make up for the disappointment but in the end these were also cancelled and people were reimbursed their ticket prices. So the Franks and Mrs Lybbe Powis, in her words 'had something of a Concert and the Sight of Madame Catalane at least'.

Other events at the Assembly Rooms attended by the Franks included a Cotillion Ball and Mr King's Benefit Ball at the Upper Rooms on the 18th April.[170] There are six references to plays in the cash book; one is worthy of note: 'Play Mrs F & self 10/d.' If that was the evening they attended the performance at the Theatre Royal it was Mr Gomery's benefit night and the evening's performance was extensive. The first item was a comedy called 'A Cure for heartache' after which Mr Gattie sang a song entitled 'THE DISAPPOINTMENT IN BATH: or a Trip to Catalani's concert' no doubt a reference to the disappointing concert in March. Catalani had her critics

169 *Bath Journal* 7/3/1808, p. 3c.
170 *Bath Chronicle* 7/4/1808, p.3b.

who claimed she added, when not ill, too much ornamentation to her singing and employed too many exuberant vocal tricks and so she was perhaps easy to caricature; though the general public loved her performances. Mr Lovegrove then sang 'The Alamanack Maker' and the final item in the evening was Mr Gomery as 'The Clown' in 'Mother Goose' when he performed for the first time his 'Grandmother's dance in pattens'.[171]

Madame Catalani's sore throat became part of Bath folklore. Richard Warner gave her the pseudonym of 'Madame Catsqualli' while telling the tale of her 'indisposition' in his 1808 satire 'Bath Characters'.[172] The sore throat also featured in a later comical account of 'A Week in Bath' published in 1811.

'Concerto a la Catalani' Thomas Rowlandson: Yale Center for British Art, Paul Mellon Collection.

This night there's a concert and there if you're willing,
To pay for your music a bit and a shilling,
You'll find all the fiddlers and singers of note,
And hear Catalani – has got a sore throat.[173]

171 *Bath Journal* 18/4/1808, p.3c.

172 Warner op. cit, p.87 et seq. Warner claims that many of the audience were very disappointed and angry with Rauzzini the concert organiser and they were only calmed by the interjection of 'Signiora Rattana', aka Susanna Wroughton, a good friend and patron of Rauzzini.

173 Anon (1811) *The Wonders of a Week in Bath*,op cit., pp.42-43.

Thomas Rowlandson produced a caricature making fun of Madame Catalani's singing, with a predictable play on her name, with the title 'Concerto a la Catalani'; there were many other caricatures making fun of her.

On the 11th March the Franks went to an exhibition. The previous year they had seen Mr Findlay's gem exhibition held because he was about to retire but a year later he was still in business and was exhibiting gems, his automata, and a valuable painting by Caravaggio, but this time at new premises in Union Street. Another exhibition in Union Street, mostly of paintings, had been advertised but it was probably Findlay's exhibition that the Franks went to see.

The weather must have been good on the 2nd April because the Franks paid the turnpike toll and took a ride on Lansdown. There was a payment a few days later for 'Mrs F's' rental of a gig (a light one person carriage) for £4-18-6d from 'Hensy', John Hensley a coachbuilder in Broad Street; so perhaps it was Priscilla on her own who had ridden up Lansdown turnpike. There were many miscellaneous items in the cash book including 5/-d to the poor wife of a soldier, various pieces of clothing for the servants, 'kesymeere' [Cashmere] gaiters for Jacob and bordered handkerchiefs for Priscilla.

The last entry on the last page of the cash book is for 26th April 1808, it lists 'bathg 4/-, play 1/-, pickles 5/6d, Mrs Molland's rout bill £2-14s' and the purchase of a new 'acct [account] book' for 1/-, in which no doubt the expenditures for the rest of their stay in Bath and of future visits to the city would have been recorded. That cash book we do not have.

16

COLONIAL WEALTH: FROM AMERICA, WEST INDIES AND THE EAST INDIES

JACOB AND PRISCILLA Franks lived a leisured life because they were born into a wealthy family that had acquired its money as merchants in British colonies stretching from North America to the West Indies and the East Indies. By the late eighteenth century though Jacob Franks was not a merchant but a manager of his property and wealth, much of which was held in Consols and other government and East India stock.

AMERICA

ON JACOB'S SIDE of the family the money came from his grandfather Jacob Franks who went to America from London, having gone there from Hanover, and became a prominent citizen of New York. He was a business man of wide interests - general commerce, shipping, privateering and slave trading. Jacob's son, the father of the Jacob of this book, David Franks moved to Philadelphia and was very successful as a fur trader and general merchant. The Franks were even tangentially involved, as middlemen, in the ginseng trade to China.[174] Moses Franks, David's brother, was a London agent for John Sanders of Schenectady who in the 1760s and early 1770s imported fabrics, tools, hats, nails and household utensils from Britain and exported furs and ginseng that he had purchased from the Indians of the Mohawk Valley. Sanders also worked with Dirk Vanderheyden the brother of Jacob's friend David Vanderheyden of Isleworth. Most importantly however during the years leading up to the War of Independence David Franks was the Commissary for the British forces in America, supplying them lucratively with the materials and resources needed by the army. David's brother Moses Franks together

---

174 Dunn jnr., W. S. (1998) *Frontier Profit and Loss: The British Army and the Fur Trade, 1760- 1774.* p. 70.

with other leading London merchants George and James Colebrooke and Arnold Nesbitt held various government contracts for victualling Jamaica and the North American colonies and David acted as their local agent.[175] Moses remained involved with these colonial contracts into the 1760s and David would have acquired much experience at sourcing the flour, cattle and other commodities needed by the army.

David Franks was commissary during Pontiac's War of 1763 and this led him to becoming involved with attempts to acquire land to the west of the Appalachian Mountains that was considered the boundary between Colonial America and the indigenous Indian nations. The context was that the British authorities had restricted the colonial traders' practice of gift giving to the Indian tribes, gifts that the Indians regarded as their payment for allowing the British to trade in their lands, and also restricted the amount of gunpowder and ammunition that the fur traders could sell to the tribes. The consequence was a war in the Great Lakes region in which a Chief called Pontiac was one of the leaders. The colonial British traders in the region suffered, they claimed, losses of £86,862 in goods lost, stolen or destroyed. David Franks bore the greatest losses and he and the other traders determined to recoup them by claiming land in Ohio country westwards and beyond the Appalachian boundary. In search of this goal Sir William Johnson the British Superintendent of Indian affairs, who was also a trader on his own account, together with David Franks and the other traders negotiated the Treaty of Stanwix with the Iroquois Confederacy in 1763. This extended the border westwards from the Appalachians to the Ohio River making it possible for Franks and his associates, including his son Jacob, to claim land in the region.

However these land claims in Ohio Country had to be ratified by the Crown as a Royal Proclamation by George III in 1763 had confirmed the Appalachians as the western limit of the British colonies and stated that private individuals could not purchase land from the Indians there without the approval of the British government. So the traders formed the Indiana Company to pursue ratification. David involved his sons Moses and Jacob in this project; Moses who was then living in London was particularly useful in lobbying the British government. The Iroquois had assumed that granting such vast territories would satisfy the traders' demands for land but in this they were mistaken.

David Franks also sought to acquire land beyond the Ohio River that could then be resold, which he thought would return a better profit than the

175 Pitock, Tom (2024) 'Imperial enterprise: The Franks Family Network, Commerce and British Expansion', in ben Ur, Avivia & Klooster, Wim (eds) *Jewish Entanglement in the Atlantic World*, Cornell: Cornell University Press.

desultory results of his general trading in the region.[176] William Murray an associate of David Franks had a copy of a Privy Council legal opinion by Lord Camden and Charles Yorke in 1757 that was given in relation to the East India Company. This confirmed that the East India Company could legally obtain land from the Mughal Emperor and other Indian princes by purchase and negotiation. Murray's copy referred only to 'Indian princes and governments' with no mention of the Great Mughal.[177] Murray and Franks and others took this to mean that despite the Royal Proclamation of 1763 they could legally purchase land from the indigenous Indians beyond the Appalachians. Murray went as an agent of David Franks in 1773 to Fort Kaskasia in what is now southern Illinois, where Franks already had a general store, and using his copy of the Camden-Yorke opinion as authorisation, proceeded to buy large tracts of land from the Indians even though the British commander of the Fort thought the transactions of dubious validity. Then in 1774 David Franks formed the Illinois Company to manage this property. The partners in the business included his sons Jacob and Moses Franks, his brother Moses Franks and his son-in-law Andrew Hamilton of Philadelphia. The British government were displeased when they learned of the deal and the role of Jacob and his uncle Moses in London was to lobby the government and press the Illinois Company's case.

These land speculations never paid off as the negotiations for ratification and confirmation of title dragged on for years and eventually came to little; but in later years David Franks had greater business problems. He was a loyalist during the American War of Independence and was imprisoned by the rebel forces for a time.[178] His fortune, as well as his liberty, was at risk. He was in London without funds between 1782 and 1786 living, as has been seen, at Isleworth with Jacob and Priscilla. David returned to New York in 1786 to reclaim his money and assets. In David's will Jacob was given 800 acres of his father's estates in America, as recognition of the kindness Jacob and Priscilla had shown him in London, as well a share of the remaining property

---

176 Stern op cit, pp. 100, 162, 165, 171-175. & Exline, M.C. (2013) Nicholas Cresswell's American Odyssey, 1774-1777, MA thesis, Liberty University, Virginia, p.21.

177 Many thought the opinion rescinded the 1763 proclamation. Stern, P. J. (2023) Empire Incorporated, London: The Belknap Press of the Harvard University Press, p. 176.

178 The Franks Family, https://snacooperative.org/view/70389694 The Susser Archive; JCR-UK, History of the Great Synagogue, Chp. 5, 'Moses Hart's School, 1722, https://www.jewishgen.org.uk/susser/roth/chfive.htm.

as tenant-in-common with his siblings. When David Franks died in 1793 he was still working to recover assets lost by being on the loyalist losing side of the American War of Independence; and it is not clear how much of his American property and wealth he had regained or managed to remit to Britain but the Franks family had gained much wealth over the years from David Franks' long and varied career as a merchant.

A slightly garbled item[179] in an eighteenth century newspaper gossip column says that Jacob claimed the great wealth of his relative Mrs Judith Levy of Richmond who died intestate. Judith Levy was the daughter of Moses Hart a London merchant and stock broker and the widow of Elias Levy a diamond merchant and government contractor. Both her husband and her father died in the 1750's and she took on running the family businesses and also became a great socialite and philanthropist.[180] Stern the modern historian also claims that Jacob received Levy's great wealth but Daiches-Dubens in her article on the Jews of Richmond says that Levy's wealth was unclaimed and remained so into modern times. The truth is that Priscilla Franks as Judith Levy's next-of-kin was granted Letters of Administration[181] to dispose of her aunt's estate in February 1803; and so she would have inherited Judith Levy's wealth.

INDIA

PRISCILLA'S FAMILY MONEY came from her father Aaron Franks who was one of the wealthiest diamond merchants in London.[182] Dealing in diamonds was a family business that Aaron had inherited from his father Abraham. The diamonds were imported from India and were paid for by

---

179 *Evening Mail* 21/2/1803, p.2c. The article mistakenly refers to Mr not Mrs Levy and to Mr Franks of Fulham not Isleworth, Stern, op cit, p164 , Daiches-Dubens, op cit, p. 156.

180 Endelman, T. M. 92004) 'Levy, Judith 1706-1803', *Oxford Dictionary of National Biography*, Oxford: Oxford University Press.

181 Letters of Administration granted to Priscilla Franks, London Metropolitan Archives, ACC/0775/790.

182 Fischel, Water, J. (1960) 'The Jewish Merchant Colony in Madras (Fort St George) during the seventeenth and eighteenth centuries: A Contribution to the Economic & Social History of the Jews in India', *Journal of the Economic and Social History of the Orient*, Vol. 3, no. 2 (August) pp. 175-195. Winder, R. (2010) *Bloody foreigners: The Story of Immigration in Britain*, Hachette, pp.116-117. Wolf, Lucien, Jews and the Coral Trade', *Transactions & Miscellanies', (Jewish History Society of England)* Vol.1, pp. xxxvi-xli, 1925.

Diamant myn

Mine de Diamans, aux Indes Orientales.

A Diamond Mine at Golconda, 1725: a romanticised view : Alamy.

silver and coral sent out from London. The coral, which was in great demand in India, was brought to London from Italy and then, under license from the East India Company, sent to Madras [Chennai]. With the proceeds from the sale of the coral, and with the imported silver, the Jewish merchant families of Madras bought diamonds from the Golconda mines in the territories of the Nizam of Hyderabad to be exported to Britain. In 1725 the ship 'Lynn' brought to Madras a consignment of coral beads valued at £2,000 and silver bullion valued at £4,000 sent from a group of Jewish London merchants, including Abraham Franks, and under the terms of their licence from the East India Company the proceeds from their sale of the coral could only be invested in diamonds and diamond boarts (chips); the Madras Jewish merchants who managed the transactions were Marcus Moses, Abraham Solomons and Aaron Franks.[183] Aaron Franks had been sent by his father to Madras in 1715, aged nineteen, to be the family's representative there and he would have lived in Coral Merchant Street in George Town, part of what was then known as Black Town just outside the walls of Fort St George. Aaron Franks remained in India until 1728[184] when he returned to Britain and became an important London based diamond dealer. The supply of coral into London was dominated by Sephardic Jewish merchants and as an Ashkenazi Jew Aaron Franks had no direct access to this trade but the Franks were on good terms with the Sephardic Franco family who originated from Leghorn [Livorno] in Italy, which allowed him to acquire the coral needed to finance his diamond purchases.[185] The Franco's family firm of Jacob, Moses and Raphael Franco, the father and two sons, had its offices at Fenchurch Street in London but the Franco's were neighbours as well as business associates of Aaron Franks. In 1778 Raphael Franco was living at Lacy House at Isleworth but when his uncle David Franco died in that year he moved to his uncle's house of Marble Hill on the Thames.

In 1724 when Aaron Franks was still in Madras the Franks family imported 38% of the diamonds that arrived in London from India. That percentage had reduced to 14% by 1730[186] but the Franks, both Aaron and his nephew Naphtali, continued importing diamonds even after 1743 when Brazil became a new source of diamonds and their prices in Europe dropped.

183   Cotton, J. J. (1945) *List of Inscriptions on Tombs & Monuments at Madras*, Madras: Government Printing Press, vol. 1.p.162.

184   Fischel, Water, J. op cit.. Yogev, Gedalia (1978) *Diamonds and Coral: Anglo-Dutch Jews and Eighteenth century Trade,* Leicester: Leicester University Press, p. 152.

185   Yogev op. cit. p. 156-158.

186   Yogev op cit. p.153

Exports of diamonds to Aaron Franks, London, 1747 -1751[187]
'Register of diamonds and precious stones to be shipped in return for coral and silver and other accounts:
Deputy Governor, Fort St David'.

Date of HEIC licence	Diamonds sent from Madras by:	To be delivered in London to:	No. of bulses [Purses of diamonds]	Value in pagodas – fanams – cash (1 pagoda = 8s – 9d in 1799)	To be transported on the ship
May 1747	Solomon Salomon – in return for a chest of coral beads	Aaron Franks & David Salomons	I bulse	700 – 0 - 0	Britannia
Feb 1747/8	Solomon Salomon	Aaron Franks	1 bulse	899 -21-63	Warwick
ditto	Solomon Salomon	Aaron Franks & David Salomons	2 bulses	6840 – 0 - 0	Warwick
Oct. 1748	Solomon Salomon	Aaron Franks & David Salomons	1 bulse	3000 -0-0	Swift
Jan 1748/9	Solomon Salomon	Aaron Franks & David Salomons	2 bulse	5538 – 27 - 73	Lapwing
Oct 1749	Solomon Salomon	Aaron Franks	1 bulse	3287 -17 – 0	Chesterfield
Sept 1750	Solomon & Moses Salomon– in part return for a chest of coral beads	Aaron Franks	1 bulse	779 – 5 - 13	Lapwing

187   Macqueen, P. (ed) (1932) *Records of Fort St George (despatches to England) 1746-1751*, Madras.pp. 20. 45, 49, 51,75, 81, 122, 177, 178.

Sept 1750	Solomon & Moses Salomon	Aaron Franks & David Salomons	2 bulses	7254 – 4 - 10	Lapwing
Feb 1750/1	Solomon & Moses Salomon – in return for the remains of a chest of coral beads	Aaron Franks	1 bulse	1749 -26 - 8	Norfolk

Solomon Salomon arrived in Madras in 1739; David Salomon was his brother and their father Abraham Salomon died in Madras in 1745. Aaron Franks was probably related to the Salomons through Benedictus Salomon the husband of his sister Abigail.

On occasion Solomon Salomons would send Aaron textiles as a present; Indian textiles were much prized in England. On the Warwick in 1748 he sent one piece of long cloth, 2 pieces of Beetela Cambrick (a fine, thin white muslin), one piece of dimity and one piece of red handkerchief.

Although Aaron Franks was not a major player in the diamond business by 1750, Aaron's bulses on the 'Warwick' in 1748 were only three in a total of 71, it was still an important part of his business. In common with the other diamond merchants in the 1750s he largely dispensed with exporting coral as a mean of remitting money to Madras and instead used a new method of remittance that was less prone to price fluctuation and was independent of the East India Company. The Company allowed its officials and military officers cargo space on board the East Indiamen sailing between Britain and India which they could use to transport goods for their own private commercial benefit. One such commodity was Madeira wine that could be obtained at Funchal on the voyage out. But the officials mostly needed a loan to purchase their stock. To meet this need Franks and the other diamond merchants gave respondentia loans. These were a commercial loan to be used to buy stock and also a form of marine insurance. When the vessel arrived safely in India the officials had to repay the loan with interest although if the cargo were lost at sea then nothing was to be repaid. The diamond merchants carried the insurance risk but the interest rates were set at such a level that the premiums repaid in India provided the cash to buy diamonds.[188]

188   Yogev op. cit. p..126-129.

The use of respondentia loans suggests that Aaron Franks was probably more widely involved in financial services. He certainly provided loans to the East India Company in 1747. At that time Britain and France were engaged in the War of Austrian Succession and the hostilities extended to India. In 1747 a French Fleet under La Bourdonnais captured Madras from the East India Company. La Bourdonnais did not take complete possession of the colony, against the wishes of Dupleix the French Governor in South India, but instead entered into ransom negotiations with Governor Morse and the Madras governing Council. They paid a large sum to protect the colony from plunder and an extra 100,000 pagodas to La Bourdonnais for his own private use. The Governor raised the money on bonds from the Jewish diamond merchants in the town, including Aaron Franks. The war ended in 1748 and Madras was returned to the East India Company; however by 1753 the Company refused to honour bonds worth 88,000 pagodas held by the Jewish merchants including Aaron Franks. The Company argued that Morse had paid the private ransom to La Bourdonnais to protect his private property and that of the other council members and not to protect the Company's property; and consequently they would not honour the bonds. Franks and the other bond holders argued that they had been led to believe that the money was paid as 'a douceur or present on behalf of the East India Company with a view to reduce the amount of the ransom insisted upon by the said Monsieur de La Bourdonnais and not to prevent private property being seized or plundered'.[189] The outcome of the case is not known but it reinforces the claim that Aaron Franks' wealth was deeply connected with the East India Company.

The involvement with the East India Company led to another aspect of Aaron's business; he was a major investor in the East Indiamen ships that were chartered by the East India Company to voyage between Britain, India and China. As early as 1729 only a few years after his return to Britain he was involved in marine insurance of ships travelling east to India and China. One surviving document is a bottomry bond for the East Indiaman the Dawson as it prepared to leave the Thames for India. Bottomry was a form of insurance similar to respondentia loans only in this case the collateral was not cargo but the ship itself. The owners would take a bottomry loan that could be used during the voyage if for example the vessel needed repairs during the journey; if it successfully returned to the Thames then the loan would be paid back

189   Birdwood, g. (1891) *Report on the Old Records of the India Office; Supplementary Notes & Appendices*, London & Calcutta, 2nd. reprint, p. 247. Aaron Franks was not in Madras at this time so presumably the bond was accepted on his behalf by his local attorneys.

together with a relatively high rate of interest. In the case of the Dawson the vessel returned safely and the money was paid to Aaron Franks.[190] Between 1739 and 1759 Aaron Franks was more directly involved in East Indian shipping and became an investor in 24 such vessels. In 1763 Aaron Franks was described as a 'very honest man tho' a Jew, [ ] who has a very great interest in the East India Company'.[191] David Franks probably took advantage of his uncle Aaron Franks' East Indian trade connections because he sometimes advertised goods from the East Indies for sale at his store in Philadelphia.

In 1777 Aaron Franks bought a one third share in the Duckenfield Hall sugar plantation in the parish of St Thomas-in-the-East in Jamaica from Sir George Colebrooke, one-time Chairman of the East India Company. The other two shares belonged to Moses Franks (Aaron's nephew and Isabella Cooper's father) and Arnold Nesbitt both of whom, together with Colebrooke, had been partners in various business activities including government contracts for provisioning the American colonies. Duckenfield was not far from the small town of Bath in St Thomas-in-the-East which was famed in Jamaica for its restorative natural hot springs and presumably was named after the

A View of the Bath Hot Spring.
Publish'd as the Act directs, July 1, 1774.

The Hot Springs at Bath, Jamaica after Paul Sandby, 1774: Permission of the Trustees of the British Museum.

190   A bottomry bond, a lot in an auction sale at Chorley's Auctioneers, 20.3.2024, lot 814.

191   Woolf, Maurice (1970-73) 'Eighteenth century Jewish Shipowners' *Transactions & Miscellanies (Jewish History Society of England)* Vol. 24, p. 199.

more famous hot springs of the city of Bath? Aaron Franks' share became the property of Priscilla Franks on her father's death. In addition Priscilla inherited much else of her father's wealth including Isleworth House.

In about 1802 Mr Arnold Nesbitt the third shareholder in the plantation went bankrupt and Priscilla's husband Jacob took on the consigneeship of the whole plantation, meaning that he was effectively in control of the entire estate. By the 1820s after her husband's death Priscilla Franks was the sole owner of the estate. None of the Franks ever visited Jamaica; the day-today management of the plantation was in the hands of trustees, attorneys and overseers.

THE WEST INDIES: THE DUCKENFIELD HALL ESTATE
AND ITS ENSLAVED PEOPLE

THERE IS SURVIVING correspondence that John Kelly, the Franks' attorney who was managing the Duckenfield estate in Jamaica, sent to Jacob Franks between 1809 and 1810, that together with other documents, allows us to review this one source of the Franks' wealth in more detail and to explore Jacob Franks' attitude towards managing a sugar plantation. Kelly wrote his letters from Green Castle estate which was a 'pen', a Jamaican term for a livestock farm, in St Thomas-in-the-East parish, that he owned and ran in addition to managing Duckenfield estate. The day to day management of

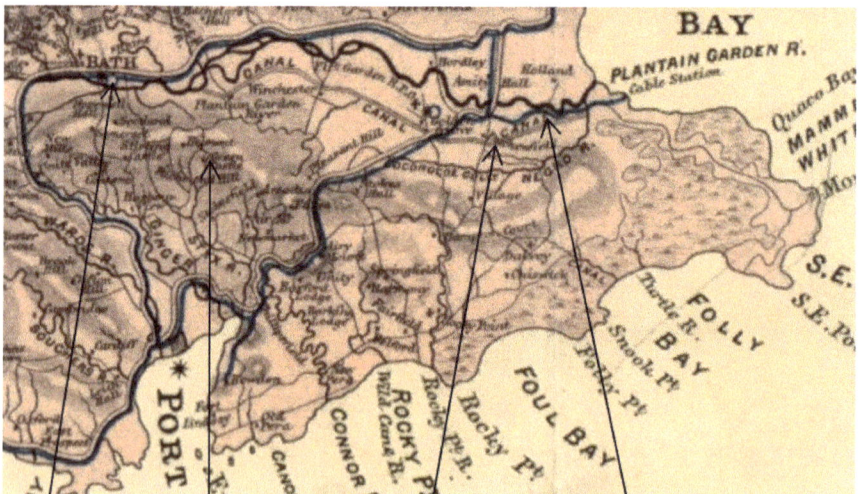

Bath   Green Castle Pen   Duckenfield Hall   Plantain Garden River

Map of St Thomas in the East parish, Surrey, Jamaica, 1862: courtesy of the Look & Learn Historical Picture Library.

Duckenfield was in the hands of an overseer. Jacob's letters to Kelly do not survive but John Kelly's replies to him make it possible to discern Jacob Franks' approach to the estate's management.

It is not known how much the Franks earned from the Duckenfield estate but an indication of its magnitude can be discerned from an indenture of 1822. Jacob Franks' nephew Jacob Henry Franks was a mortgagee of the estate, probably an investment to provide him with an income, and between October 1805 and August 1822 he was paid on average interest of £1,778 per annum. It is likely that the Franks were receiving at least as much as their nephew if not more. However by the 1800s profits from sugar plantations were much less than the 10% return that had been common in the first half of the eighteenth century.[192]

Economy and retrenchment of costs were Jacob's overriding concern. In December Kelly was dealing with Jacob's responses to the annual list of goods and supplies he had asked to be sent to Jamaica. Little had escaped Jacob's attention forcing Kelly to write:

> I must own that the words damask prefixed to the table cloth and mahogany to the beds had escaped my observation when I was examining the list. If they had not I should certainly have struck them out, and in that case perhaps you might not have thought the table cloths and beds too expensive and objectionable.

Jacob also queried the cost of fine gunpowder suspecting it was to enable Kelly and the overseer to enjoy field sports at his expense. Kelly replied that it was for the cartridges that 'a quantity of which in proportion to each white man on it, the estate is bound by law to provide. It most certainly is not to shoot with for the Overseer is as little a sportsman as I am and for my part I never shot a bird in my life and never wished to do so'. The overseer was obviously viewed by Jacob as a man too willing to live over-comfortably at Jacob's expense.

> The Overseer says he will never send for porter, ale and cheese again, but in my opinion a reasonable quantity of them ought to be allowed to the estate as they are an encouragement to the white people who seeing other estates get such things would think it hard not to get them too.

---

192 Ward, J. R. (1978) 'The profitability of Sugar plantations in the British West Indies', *Economic History Review*, Vol. 31, No. 2.

Franks' frugality towards the overseer does seem rather grudging given his habit of sending many cheeses to friends and family whenever he was in Bath.

Kelly had suggested that the enslaved workers on Duckenfield estate should be given clothing more often but Franks' response over the increased costs only caused him to reiterate the benefits of so doing. Kelly wrote:

> The great increase is certainly in the clothing… At the Duckenfield estate the negroes during crop keep spell[193] every other night and their houses are at a considerable distance from the marks. This gives them a long walk at night and in the wet weather the labour is particularly severe on them. To keep them warmly clothed therefore must be a great benefit to them.

It seems that Kelly had informed Franks that there was a particular estate that clothed its workers twice a year, to which Franks had obviously replied that just because one did so did not imply that Duckenfield should do so. So Kelly explained that he 'instanced that [estate] because I know the good effects there', and that indeed clothing twice a year was common practice on the island. Franks had asked Kelly whether he provided his own enslaved people at Green Castle pen with extra clothing. He replied that his was a stock rearing estate and not one that produced sugar and consequently:

> With regard to my own negroes they are very differently circumstanced from those of sugar estates. The few of them that are occasionally sent out to job,[194] never keep spell as it is customary for jobbers so to do. By far the greater part of them never stir off the property where they have comparatively speaking very light work to do all the year round. Add to this that throughout the whole of each year they get their days regularly to cultivate their provision ground by which they are enabled to sell provisions, besides what they keep for use, and the money they receive for which, they expend in buying extra clothing for themselves. Now negroes on other sugar estates generally have no days allowed them.[195]

Although it was true that sugar cultivation was the toughest type of agricultural labour it is unlikely that Kelly's enslaved workforce who avoided

---

193   An American usage meaning a turn of labour.

194   A job and jobbing was when enslaved people were sent to do contract work outside of the plantation that owned them. There were also jobbers who were enslaved people owned by gang masters not attached to any particular estate who hired them out as casual labour to plantations.

195   Letter from Kelly to Franks, dated 28/10/1809, ACC 775 928/1.

that particular burden regarded their work as 'very light'.

When the supplies arrived Kelly was disappointed that there was no provision for additional clothing and he wrote to Franks

> The promise of this pennistone[196] would have furnished the negroes with a second service of good warm clothing in the crop times. In the next list of supplies I will again submit to you the propriety of sending out a sufficiency of pennistone for that purpose, but in other respects, I trust you will think it [the list] as moderate as it ought to be.[197]

And he did, the next list included many yards of blue baize, oznaburg and other textiles.[198] However unlike the enslaved people who had not received a 'second service of good warm clothing' the overseer was 'very well pleased to get his beer and cheese'.

Kelly was always pre-empting Franks' worry about costs. When he increased the request for 90 barrels of herring (used to provision the enslaved people on the estate), he added that if they could be sent from Glasgow that would save on costs. Apart from Kelly's attempts to persuade Jacob that he was doing all he could to keep costs down the correspondence deals with many issues concerning the estate's production of sugar, rum and bananas. The weather and hurricanes were a frequent problem; in 1809 the Plantain Garden River flooded the cane fields and the mill was shut down for three days whilst the enslaved labour force repaired the damage caused by the waters. The practicalities of shipping the estate's produce to Britain were always a concern and insurance had to be negotiated and bought. Much of the correspondence dealt with the arrivals, departures and delays of shipping. Even when the cargoes reached Britain there were sometimes problems. Jacob Franks complained that one consignment of rum was cloudy. Kelly replied:

> As for the rum being cloudy, I promise you one's aware that a certain quantity of burnt sugar is put in each purchase to colour it. Now cloudiness may have proceeded from something in the sugar, with which the rum was coloured or

196 Pennystone / pennistone / penistone – a cheap, coarse woollen cloth dyed with indigo woven in Yorkshire and generally exported for clothing for enslaved people in the West Indies. The Penistone cloth –Textiles & slavery;https://britishtextilebiennial.co.uk/programme/the-penistone-cloth/. Other textiles used for plantation clothing included oznaburg, a coarse linen and baize.

197 Letter from Kelly to Franks, dated 10/3/1810 , ACC 775 928/7.

198 Letter from Kelly to Franks, ACC 775/ 928/17 & 27/4/1810, ACC 775 928/15.

from the casks themselves. It was certainly clear when in the butts in the rum store.[199]

He promised he would make sure that the next batch was properly coloured.

Kelly also reported to Franks on regional politics and affairs. He was annoyed in 1809 because the Junta de Seville that governed Spanish West Indies had closed Cuba to all foreign vessels, as part of its opposition to France. Cuba was where Kelly had bought 'tolerably priced' staves for making barrels. He was puzzled why the Junta did not make an exception for British vessels as Britain had expended 'treasure and blood' fighting the common foe Napoleonic France. To make good the short fall he sent the estate's carpenters to make staves from the estate's own woodland but the stock of suitable trees was nearly depleted. He bought other staves cheaply from a vessel that had been shipwrecked on the coast but still had to buy a further 2,500 staves.

Jacob Franks' inclination was to become closely involved in the management of Duckenfield but with the distance between Isleworth and the plantation this was impracticable; it could take several weeks for letters to arrive and multiple copies had to be sent on different packet ships as letters could easily be lost. Nevertheless Kelly was obliged to respond to all Franks' detailed concerns and worries.

In January 1822 when Priscila Franks became sole owner of the Duckenfield Hall there were 228 enslaved people on the estate, 110 men and 118 women, according to the 'schedule of slaves'.[200] This was 53 fewer than the number in 1810. Even in 1810 Jacob Franks was worried about the declining number of enslaved people on the estate. Kelly wrote:

> I observe what you say about the women not breeding at the estate. In former years they bred in the usual proportion but in 1809 only one child was reared tho' many women were pregnant who miscarried at the early stages of their pregnancy.

---

199   Letter from Kelly to Franks, dated16/2/1809, ACC775/928/4.

200   London Metropolitan Archives, Schedule of slaves on Duckenfield Hall plantation in 1822, attached to an indenture, Acc/0775/868. The indenture concerned a mortgage on the estate held by Priscilla's nephew Jacob Henry Franks who also signed the schedule. Smith, R. W. (1950) 'Slavery and Christianity in the British West Indies', *Church History,* Vol. XIX, no. 3. University College London, (UCL) Centre for the Study of the Legacies of British Slavery, Priscilla Franks http://wwwdepts-live.ucl.ac.uk/lbs/person/view/-535810822. Accessed 30/11/2022 Duckenfield Hall, Jamaica, St Thomas-in-the-East, Surrey http://wwwdepts-live.ucl.ac.uk/lbs/estate/view/3249 Accessed 30/11/2022.

This decline in births in Franks' eyes meant that his capital stock was not being replenished. Kelly then went on to give his explanation about the general problem of the declining size of the enslaved population in Jamaica. From Kelly's colonial Christian perspective he thought it was to do with polygamous sexual relations.

> Almost all the estates in the parish have fallen off in numbers, since the abolition of the slave trade and three years' experience has fully convinced us here, if indeed that had at all been previously necessary, that the Black population cannot be kept up without importation from Africa. The habits of the negroes themselves are against their natural population increase as it might otherwise do. The men universally engage in Polygamy but they are not solely to blame for I am fairly convinced it would be infinitely easier to convince the men to give up that practice than to prevail on the women to confine themselves each to their own husband. Plus in truth the Sword cuts both ways, as the dissoluteness in both sexes impedes propagation'.[201]

In 1810 the slave trade had been abolished but slavery had not and the system of plantations was under threat as the supply of enslaved people diminished. The thinking of Kelly, and probably many planters in Jamaica, was so enmeshed with slavery that they saw the problem as with the enslaved people and not with the system of slavery. There is an unarticulated mechanism implied in Kelly's analysis; he either believed that polygamy somehow reduced the chance of pregnancy, Doctors at that time thought frequent sex could reduce fertility, or that women with several partners were more likely to attempt contraception or to seek abortions. Much of the decline in fertility amongst the enslaved population however was probably due to the harsh working conditions and poor diet that the women endured.

The theme of enslaved women managing their fertility underlies Kelly's report on the particular causes of the increase in miscarriages on the Duckenfield estate; but he did not consider their motivations for doing so.

THE DECLINE IN THE BIRTH RATE — DIFFERENT PERSPECTIVES

Kelly thought that on the Duckenfield estate there was a more specific reason for the decline in the birth rate in recent years.

201   Letter from Kelly to Franks, dated 7/9/1810. ACC 775/928/17

We only have, through Kelly's letter, his view of what was happening but an empathetic imagining of the story from the perspective of the enslaved hints at a very different reading. Kelly wrote:

> I was struck with the circumstances [of so few live births] and initiated a strict enquiry into the business when I discovered that a worthless Old Woman who had long been eyeing up the negroe houses was partly instrumental in frightening the pregnant women in which she was seconded by her son who was the Head Driver on the estate. This is what the women themselves alleged to me, have given rise to their frequent miscarriages. As for the Old Womans motives they took their [rise ?], partly from a wish to please her son, and partly from an inhuman and wicked disposition. Some strange and curious reasons were given for the conduct of the son, in his part of the transaction. Upon making of this discovery I instantly broke the Head Driver and placed another, and I think better disposed man in his room and I threatened the Old Woman with giving her over to the Laws of the Country. There is reason to flatter myself that these numerous moves have been effective, for there are now nine women pregnant on the estate and in a fair way of doing well.[202.]

What could have been the motives of the head driver and his mother? Some historians have suggested that control of fertility and abortion were a form of resistance to slavery by denying plantations the future labour supply they required.[203] It was thought by the Europeans in Jamaica that obeah men and women who practised traditional African religion and medicine knew about powders and herbs that could induce abortion. Perhaps the 'Old Woman' was such a practitioner and she and her son were seeking to undermine the plantation by encouraging and helping pregnant women on the estate to end their pregnancy by spells, incantation and, more effectively, by herbal preparations that could end a pregnancy (whether the herbs used were effective in this is not known)? Or perhaps women simply did not want to have children who would be bound to a life

---

202   Ibid.

203   Clover, David (2008) ' "This horably wicked action" abortion and resistance on a Jamaican slave plantation', Society of Caribbean Studies Annual Conference, pp, 4 & 6. http://www.caribbeanstudies.org.uk/papers/vol9.htm

of slavery. Kelly clearly believed that the problem arose because of the machinations of the Head Driver and his mother; he did not consider that the women might have been fully complicit as a form of protest. However this can only be speculation, the minds of the enslaved women on the Duckenfield estate cannot be known.

Baptist, Methodist and Moravian missionaries had for many years been actively evangelising the enslaved population of Jamaica. The 'schedule of slaves' for Duckenfield gives the 'original' pre-baptism names, Christian names, ages, occupations and states of health of all the enslaved people. Some of their pre-baptism names were standard Christian names such as Sarah and William some were belittling such as 'Present' (Margaret Thompson), 'Trial' (Robert Francis) the cooper and 'Hard Times', who was the estate's fisherman and was one of the few who had not been baptised. A number of the people had the surname Nesbitt that referred to an earlier owner of the Duckenfield estate. A few had the surname Franks, William Franks (Bob) was the 3rd Head Driver, Edward Franks aged 83 was an invalid and Jacob Franks was a shepherd. The planters were generally against baptism of their enslaved people but could not prevent it. Later they believed their opposition was justified by the extensive rebellion in Jamaica in 1831 that was led by Christian enslaved people and was known as the Baptist rebellion.

The religious beliefs amongst the enslaved people of Jamaica however were a syncretic mixture of Christian beliefs and the African religious practises mentioned earlier known as Obeah that involved both spell casting and traditional herbal medicine. These practices were seen by the colonialists as a hidden form of combination by the blacks and a conspiracy and threat to white supremacy in the island. Colonialists mostly live a culturally parallel but distinct and separate life from that of the colonised resulting in a constant anxiety that they are ignorant of how the colonised may be plotting and organising. This was certainly the case amongst the Jamaican planters and so unsurprisingly Obeah was made illegal in 1760. Gloucester an enslaved man from Duckenfield was tried for practising Obeah and was hanged in January 1814.[204] He would have treated the illnesses of the enslaved people on Duckenfield, cast spells and provided fetishes to protect them from harm even though most of them had been baptised.

The enslaved work force on the plantation in 1822 was organised hierarchically and functionally. John Rochford (Busy) was the Head Driver

204 *Royal Gazette of Jamaica*, 29/1/1814.

or foreman, and the several different functions within the plantation each had its own head together with a number of assistants. On Duckenfield these included Thomas Nesbitt head wainman or waggoner, with four wainmen, William Holmes head carpenter, with five carpenters and Natty Roberts the head mason who had one other mason working for him. Rum was a major product of the plantation and was produced by William Martin the head distiller. Robert Sandford was the head cooper and had seven coopers working for him who made the barrels. Other men were field workers who at different times also worked in the sugar factory and the distillery.

Among the women Lizzy Sergeant aged 31 was the bookkeeper but she was 'weakly'. Penny James, formerly Affra, was a 'Doctress' who tended injured or ill enslaved people. Most of the enslaved women however were field workers who cultivated the sugar cane or were engaged in other farm work such as looking after the fowl house or, as did Mary Ann Brown, cleaning out the hog pen.

The field workers were divided into the great gang, the men who undertook the heaviest field work, the second gang of women and less fit men who did the less arduous fieldwork and the small gang including children and the capable invalids who did menial work such as weeding. Much of the most heavy work on Jamaican plantations such as preparing the square 'marks' and digging the holes for planting the canes, was done by jobbing gangs. These were enslaved men who were not attached to any plantation but were owned

Sugar cane cultivation showing the preparation of marks and squares: Alamy.

by a master who hired them out to plantations as casual labour. Their work was arduous and they were often under the fiercest discipline. Plantation owners used jobbers as a way to boost productivity and also to protect the health of their own enslaved labour. However it seems that in 1809 Jacob Franks thought it an unnecessary expense to pay to bring in labour when the plantation had its own resident workforce. John Kelly wrote:

> With regard to economy generally speaking of carrying on the business of the estate I have such necessity as firmly rooted in my mind as you could wish for and accordingly I have, I am, doing, everything in my power to retrench on this side of the water as much as I possibly can consistently with the [illegible] cultivation and general good of the estate. You are already aware of the great reduction of jobbing which is now confined to about the annual level that I understand you to approve of.

In another letter written a couple of months previously he reported that there had been no jobbers on the estate recently. The implication was that the estate's own enslaved labour would have to work harder to cover the absence of jobbers. But still Franks complained if he saw anything in the accounts that suggested money was being wasted employing outside labour. He wrote in October 1810 querying the £24 -10s-1d that had been paid to someone to supervise the working women. Kelly again had to explain the situation;

> The charge of £24-10s-1d for superintending the women negroes was in fact an error in the wording committed by [the clerk?]. The person was employed by the estate and has now been discharged.[205]

Often in his letters Kelly lets slip a sublimated exasperation at Franks' micromanagement from a distance. Nevertheless Kelly frequently sent his best wishes to Mrs Franks, Priscilla, in April 1810 for example he wrote 'Thanks to Mrs Franks for the preserves she was good enough to send me.[206]

Each of the enslaved gangs had its own cook, Mary Waters (Red Esther) for the great gang, Eleanor Lindsay (Sarah) for the small gang and Johannah [illegible] (Coco) for the 2nd Gang, Susan McDowell (Catherine) was house cook, presumably catering for the estate overseer's household who lived in the plantation house. There were twenty three children aged under the age of eight on the estate which seems to have been the age at which

205 Letter from Kelly to Franks, dated 5/10/1810. ACC 775/928/18.

206 Letter from Kelly to Franks, dated 27/4/1810, ACC/775/928/9.

children were set to work. Five of the children were still 'at the breast'. There were two runaways listed, one had gone as many years before as 1803, but he was still listed as an estate asset. A few years after the schedule was drawn up William Nesbitt, a 'creole' who was a field worker in 1822 later became a mason and then absconded in 1826. He had been given a pass in July but never returned to the estate until he was apprehended and detained at St Elizabeth's workhouse.[207]

JACOB FRANKS AND THE ENSLAVED WORKERS' HOUSING

It was clearly John Kelly's view that Jacob Franks' comments were based on little knowledge of Jamaica or of sugar plantations. By 1810 Franks owned an English country estate in Norfolk but if he thought this similar to managing a sugar plantation Kelly was keen to disabuse him. In a letter to Franks he had mentioned building new houses for the estate's enslaved workers and Franks had queried this. Kelly again sought to explain.

I have read with infinite concern what you have said on the subject of the building and repairing of negroe houses, which you observed was [illegible] on looking into the journal sent you in my letter of July. But it appears to me that you are under a misapprehension with regard to this affair. I trust that the explanation, which I shall now take the liberty of giving you on that point will remove the unfavourable thoughts which at present you appear to entertain with regard to it. From the term building "new negroe houses" I conclude that you are of the opinion that such houses are built in this country somewhat in the same manner and at the same expense as farm houses are built in England; and from what you say about a new trash house[208] (which is an estate building) that you had no idea that other buildings were wanted, thus classing negroe houses with estate buildings properly so called, I am the more confirmed in this opinion. But in reality all estate negroe houses are built of such materials, and in such a manner, as to repeatedly require some repairs and in the progress

207 *Royal Gazette of Jamaica*, 28/10/1826, p. 18b.

208 A trash house was used for storing and drying the used sugar cane so that it could later be used as a fuel in the sugar factory. The old trash house was carried away in the flood of 1809, letter dated 16/12/1809, ACC 928/4.

Nineteenth century huts for enslaved people: Alamy.

of time to be put up anew. And in consequence it is always generally usual after crop time to give the assistance of the carpenters to do such jobs at the negroes' houses and this is such a matter of course that I thought you were well aware of it and therefore did not in particular specify it in my letter to you. Now as to the expense allow me to reassure you that absolutely no positive expense was the estate put to but in the few nails used in the repairs of the houses, and the few feet of common white pine boards used in repairing old doors and windows, and where necessary making new ones. And not only was the expense of both very trifling indeed, in effect, but surely it was not an amount to be put in competition with the great satisfaction it was, and is, to the negroes to have their cottages (if they are nothing like) weather tight and comfortable exclusive of the benefits their health receives from these circumstances. And I flatter myself after the exposition of the facts as they truly are that you will concur with me on my sentiments.[209]

209   Letter from Kelly to Franks dated 16/12/1809, ACC/775/928/4.

Kelly's letters to Jacob Franks do not suggest that the latter had any interest in the health, conditions and system of discipline under which his enslaved people - his property- were living. Such things were of course important. John Kelly may have been slightly more concerned about the enslaved workforce. He had a 'natural' child named Mary Kelly with his mistress Sarah Edwards Innis, a 'free woman of colour of St Thomas-in-the-east' parish. When Kelly died in 1814 he left £1,400 to Sarah and £4,000 in trust for his daughter to be used to buy land but only if it was in Ireland, Scotland or the counties of York and Middlesex.[210]

Although in the 1822 indenture schedule Abram Room the then overseer reported, however accurately we do not know, that most of the enslaved people were healthy nineteen of them were listed as invalids. They included Betty Price (Seraphina) who was said to be 105 years old but in addition nine were listed as 'in yaws'.[211] Yaws is a skin infection, spread by skin contact that was endemic in West Indian plantations in the nineteenth century. The phrase 'in yaws' suggest that the sufferers at Duckenfield were housed in an isolation hut looked after by Susannah Smith aged 49 the 'yaws nurse'.

There was controversy at the time about the nature of yaws. It was known the disease was similar to syphilis and some argued they were the same and that both were spread by sexual contact. The slavery abolitionists claimed that the rise of syphilis in Britain had been caused by British men catching yaws in the West Indies and that this was one example of the great evils that arose from slavery. Other Europeans claimed that syphilis and yaws were not the same. The enslaved Africans knew from long community experience of the disease in West Africa that this was correct and that yaws was spread by simple contact and not specifically a sexually transmitted disease. The enslaved community often practised childhood innoculation against yaws that had long been the custom in Africa. In the nineteenth century this led to a debate on the plantations about whether European treatments (largely administering mercury) or African treatments were most effective against yaws. In this context an intriguing question about Duckenfield arises. Six of the nine people 'in yaws' were children and the remaining three were adult women aged between 19 and 43; was the yaws hut being used to innoculate the children by introducing infected matter into lesions on those being innoculated (a method

210   Centre for the Study of the Legacies of British Slavery, University College London (UCL), ucl.ac.uk/lbs.

211   Paugh, K. (2014) 'Yaws, Syphilis and Sexuality and the Circulation of Medical Knowledge in the British Caribbean and the Atlantic World', *Bulletin of the History of Medicine*, Vol. 88, no. 2 pp. 225-252.

of smallpox innoculation used in Britain), or were they simply being isolated in the yaws hut to prevent widespread contagion?

There is no specific evidence on whether the enslaved people of Duckenfield estate were treated harshly or leniently. Kelly was responsive however when a drought meant the enslaved people on the estate were 'rather scarce of provisions' and at their request he sent up some barrels of corn flour; though he then had to write to Franks, perhaps uncertainly, that 'I am certain that you will approve, I am happy to say that their scarcity can only be temporary as the season for yams will now come in very soon'.[212]

A handbook on managing plantations in Jamaica published in 1823[213] argued that the lot of enslaved people on the island had improved as a result of the abolition of the slave trade (but not of slavery), as new slaves could not be brought from Africa, and also because of local ordinances outlawing the worst of the old practices. Nevertheless the manual still argued that enslaved people were childlike, cunning and lazy and could only be managed by strict and harsh discipline. The head driver's whip was not just a badge of office. The general evidence about the treatment of enslaved people on plantations in Jamaica suggests that the Duckenfield enslaved workers would have been treated harshly and possibly cruelly using both physical punishment and psychological manipulation. The latter was achieved for instance by displaying on roadsides the heads of executed slaves and by exploiting the widespread belief in spirits and fetishes.[214] The enslaved population's resentment of their position and treatment was sufficient to trigger the uprising in Jamaica of Christian enslaved people of 1831 against the planters, the 'Baptists War' that was led by a Black Baptist deacon.

212   Letter from Kelly to Franks, dated 21/7/1810, ACC/775/928/15.

213   Roughly, T. (1823) *The Jamaica Planter's Guide or a system for planting and managing a sugar estate or other plantations in that island*, London: Longman. The British government published in 1824 Orders in Council for the amelioration of the condition of slaves in those West Indian islands that it directly governed. The measures included prohibiting the use of the whip on female slaves and its use on male slaves as a 'stimulus to labour' although it could still be used as a legitimate punishment. In his speech to the House of Commons the Foreign Secretary George Canning pointed out that Jamaica's autonomous legislature was very much opposed to such measures. Canning explicitly stated that 'negros' lacked rational and moral development and were essentially 'childlike'. *Hansard, House of Commons Debates*, 16th March 1824, Vol. 10, cc 1091-198. 'Amelioration of the Condition of the Slave Population of the West Indies'

214   Brown, Vincent (2003) 'Spiritual Terror and Sacred Authority in Jamaican Slave Society', *Slavery & Abolition*, vol. 24, No. 1, pp 24-53.

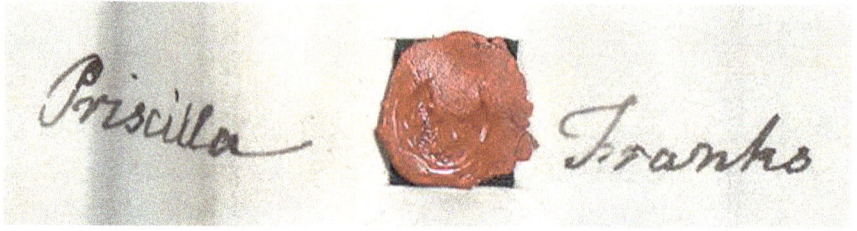

The signature and seal of Priscilla Franks on the Schedule; courtesy of the London Metropolitan Archives.

After Jacob's death Priscilla Franks was an absentee landlord and it is not known how much interest she took in the Duckenfield plantation; but it was sufficient to buy 56 new enslaved persons for the estate in 1826. After her death in 1832, two years before the abolition of slavery, the Duckenfield Hall plantation was inherited by Lady Isabella Bell Cooper. After the abolition of slavery the compensation of £6379-12s-5d for the loss of their property – the enslaved people – was awarded to Sir Henry Allen Johnson acting on behalf of Lady Cooper the beneficiary.[215] The plantation remained in Lady Cooper's possession until her death in 1855 when it went to her daughter Mrs Dawkins. It was sold in 1877.

THE FRANKS' WEALTH

WHEN HE DIED in 1814 Jacob Franks' personal wealth, excluding the capital value of his property, was £250,000,[216] when Priscilla Franks died in 1832 she left £400,000. The Franks' family wealth had its source in the leveraging of Britain's colonial position; sometimes very directly, as in the case of David Franks' role in provisioning the British army in America, not always successfully as in the instance of land speculation in the Indian territories of Ohio Country and Illinois Country but mostly profitably as for example the East India trade and the Jamaican sugar plantation. As in the Franks' case colonial wealth was often at the cost of the colonised such as the population of Bengal, much of whose wealth was remitted to Britain, the indigenous people of America, whose ancestral lands were encroached upon, and the enslaved people of the West Indies whose minds and bodies were expropriated.

215   Centre for the Study of the Legacies of British Slavery (UCL) Jamaica St Thomas-in-the-East, Surrey, 114 (Duckenfield Hall) Claim details, https://www.ucl.ac.uk/lbs/claim/view/24495.

216   Rubenstein, W. (2001) 'Jewish Top Wealth-holders in Britain, 109-1909', *Jewish Historical Studies,* Vol. 37, pp. 133-166.

17

THE FRANKS' LATER LIVES AND CONNECTIONS WITH BATH

LITTLE ELSE IS known of Jacob and Priscilla except that they continued to live at Isleworth and travelled occasionally to Bath. In January 1806 Jacob Franks 'of Isleworth' bought the house at no. 3 the Kings Circus in Bath from the estate of William Colborne for £3,800 but he then sold it in May the same year to Admiral Rainier for £4,000. The Franks never lived there; Colborne had lived at no. 3 until his death and then in 1806 it was unoccupied until Admiral Rainer moved in the following year.[217] The Franks however almost certainly continued visiting the city after 1808 but they have left no records of their visits apart from reports of Mr & Mrs Franks arriving in the city in January 1809 and of a Mr Franks in November 1810.

Jacob and Priscilla had close family who were permanent residents of Bath. Priscilla owned the house in St Catherine's Place in Bath that was leased to her sister-in-law Rebecca and her husband Sir Henry Johnson, and Andrew Hamilton her nephew was married in Bath in 1816 and then lived at Burlington Street.

In 1805 or thereabouts Jacob Franks completed his transition to becoming an English gentleman when he bought West Harling Hall and park in Norfolk. The house was built in the Palladian style in 1725; it was demolished in 1930.[218] On the 14th June 1805 he set off from Isleworth 'to view'[219] West Harling accompanied by 'Grimault', probably the Mr Grimault who was an auctioneer and valuer who worked in London and the Richmond

217 Bath City Rate Books 1799 -1807. Bath Record Office, BC/22/2/3/9/44-47.

218 There are many references in the newspapers to Grimault as an auctioneer, examples are, Morning Herald, 7/8/1806, p.4a, 27/4/1810, p.4c & Morning Advertiser, 20/3/1807, p.4c.

219 Anon (n.d.) The West Harling Hall, thedicamillo.com. Franks' travel expenses cash book, London Metropolitan Archives, ACC/775/73.

area. He then made brief return visits in July and August by which time he had obviously acquired the property[220] because in September Jacob, Priscila and the household departed from Isleworth to 'live at West Harling' for the winter. Initially the Franks took with them Liversedge, Gorla their cook-confectioner and three maids. These were later followed by Foulon the butler, three more maids, the men servants William, James, Henry, and George 'with the dogs'. Jacob was obviously intent on living a gentleman's country life. His name appears regularly from 1805 onwards in the published lists of certificates for his gamekeepers in West Harling and Larling. The Franks returned to Isleworth in January 1806. A few months later, as we have seen earlier, Jacob Franks went to Bath to consult his doctor. The travel expenses cash book ends with entries in 1809 and up until that date the Franks made regular trips to West Harling that interspersed their visits to Bath, and they sometimes spent the last quarter of the year in Norfolk. They also made other excursions; in October 1804 Jacob, Priscilla, 'AH', together with their servants William Argent and Sarah Liversedge, travelled on horseback to see Lady Cooper at her home at Little Thurlow Hall.

The culmination of Jacob Franks; social elevation was in August 1803 when he was formally introduced by his brother-in-law General Henry Johnson to King George III at Windsor.[221] As was expected of a country gentleman Jacob Franks subscribed to all the important local, national and patriotic charitable causes. In 1803 he gave £100 to the Fund for the Relief and Reward of Defenders of the Country[222] and as a Norfolk landowner he subscribed to the 1809 Fund for the Poor Sufferers from the Inundation of the Fens.[223] Two years later he gave to the Fund for the Relief of British Prisoners in France[224] and two years after that, as Napoleon's armies invaded Russia, to the relief of the inhabitants of Russian territories who had consequently suffered.[225] When Napoleon was defeated in 1815 Jacob was dead and so it was Priscilla who gave to the Waterloo Fund[226] for commemorating the victory.

Jacob Franks died at York House in Bath on the 10th May 1814; he was probably staying at his Club which by then was known as the York Club. In

220   Jacob Franks first appears in the West Harling overseers' rate book in 1805.

221   *True Briton*, 18/9/1803, p.2e.

222   *True Briton*, 10/8/1803, p.1b.

223   *Norfolk Chronicle*, 26/5/1809, p.1e.

224   *Globe*, 14/2/1811, p.1a.

225   *Star*,26/1/1813, p.1.d.

226   *The Sun*, 27/7/1815, p.1a.

his will[227] he had specified that should he die at Isleworth he should be buried at Isleworth church but should he die elsewhere he wished to be buried in the nearest parish graveyard; consequently he was buried in the burial ground of St Michael's Without in Bath [The burial ground was removed when the Hilton hotel was built]. The *Bath Chronicle* reported that 'his liberality, hospitality and goodness of heart, endeared him to a widely extended circle of friends'. He insisted however on a plain funeral without unnecessary expense and wished if he died between October and March to be buried before 9 o'clock in the morning and if in the summer months before 7 o'clock. In his will he made bequests to Anna Maria the widow of his brother Moses (the one time Chief Justice of the Bahamas), to his nephew Andrew Hamilton and his sisters, to his sister the wife of General Henry Johnson and to their son Henry Allen Johnson. There were bequests to Edward Goldsmid his long term friend and business associate and to his long serving servant William Argent, who had been with him on several of his visits to Bath; all his other personal and real property went to Priscilla. After her husband's death, Priscilla was a joint owner of the Duckenfield Hall plantation and by 1822 she was the sole owner of the estate. She was not as concerned with the country estates as Jacob had been and she sold off West Harling Hall and Park.

Priscilla Franks lived until 1832 and in her later years in her seventies and eighties she ceased from visiting Bath. Her cash book from 1824 to 1831 survives and there are no entries relating to any visits to the city.[228] The expenditure recorded was mostly servants' and household expenses; she was however paying quarterly the annuities that Jacob had made in his will and other allowances. The names of the recipients are now familiar. Sir Henry Johnson received £125 a quarter, his son's wife Mrs H. A. Johnson £50, Lady Cooper £200, Mrs A. M. Franks, probably Priscilla's sister-in-law Anna Maria Franks, £50 and the widowed Lady Honywood £200. Sir John and Lady Honywood had long been friends of the Franks; The Honywood's daughter Charlotte had married Colonel Cooper, Lady Cooper's brother-in-law in 1805. Sir John Honywood was a Member of Parliament for many years and when he died in 1806 he was succeeded by Sir John Courtney Honywood who married Mary Anne Cooper, Isabella's Cooper's eldest daughter, at Little

---

227 Will of Jacob Franks of Isleworth, 1822, National Archives, PROB 11/1557/237, *Bath Chronicle*, 12/5/1814, p.4. The grant of probate giving Duckenfield in trust to Priscilla Franks, London Metropolitan Archives, ACC/0775/787.

228 Private research report from London Metropolitan Archives concerning the 'leather book containing accounts, probably belonging to Priscilla Franks', 1824-1831. London Metropolitan Archives Ref. Acc/0775/074

Thurlow in 1808.[229] In May 1809 Jacob and Priscilla travelled from Isleworth to visit the Honywoods at their house at Evington in Kent.

Priscilla Franks died at Isleworth on the 13th November and was buried in the parish churchyard; though she had said in her will that if she died away from Isleworth she should be buried with Jacob at Bath. Like Jacob she requested a plain funeral and limited the number of carriages there should be in the funeral procession. Jacob and Priscilla had no children and the beneficiaries of her £400,000 estate included family members, Sir Henry Johnson and his son Henry Allen Johnson, Anna Maria, wife of Jacob's brother Moses Franks and Sir William Cooper the husband of Priscilla's aunt/niece (such were the complexities of the Franks' family tree) Isabella Bell Cooper.

The inclusion of Sir William Henry Cooper in Priscilla's will raises the question of what happened to William and Isabella after the Cadogan scandal. Mary Cadogan died in France in 1811 and at the end of the Napoleonic War William Henry Cooper returned to Britain where he had inherited his father's country house and estate.[230] Sometime around 1820 he sought reconciliation with Lady Isabella Cooper and the couple resumed some kind of relationship. They acquired a London house at No. 57 Portland Street and in 1833 they inherited Isleworth House from Priscilla Franks as well as the plantation in the West Indies. William Cooper soon began extensive improvements and extensions to Isleworth House and he seems to have been accepted back into polite society; his fashionable arrival at places was sometimes recorded in the newspapers.[231] The Rev Sir William Henry Cooper, to give him his full title, died in 1835 at the Portland Street house but was buried at Worlington church; Lady Isabella Bell Cooper died in 1855 and was also buried at Worlington. There is a memorial in the church to both of them and to their son William Henry, who died in 1836.

General Sir Henry and Lady Rebecca Johnson continued living in Bath.[232] Henry was an enthusiastic member of the Royal Harmonic Society into the 1820s. Rebecca Johnson died on the 14th February 1822 and was buried in St Michael's graveyard in the city. Henry remained active in Bath's

229 *Oxford Journal*, 6/8/1808, p.3b.

230 Brun, J. P. (2013) The Dawkins of Moggerhanger: a Short History, https://moggerhanger.uk/wp-content/uploads/2021/09/Dawkins-of-Moggerhanger2.pdf.

231 *Morning Post*, 8/1/1816, 25/4/1831, p.3d, Sir William Cooper Bart and Lady Cooper arrive in London, *New Times*, 8/1/1830, p. 3c.

232 References to Henry Johnson in the *Bath Chronicle*, 1/7/1807, 19/12/1811, 2/5/1824, 9/8/1827, 24/10/1824, 9/2/1826, 24/11/1831

society after his wife's death; He was one of the organisers of the Bath & Somerset Grand Musical Festival in the 1820s. He was a steward at the Grand Masked Fete[233] that the York Club, of which Jacob Franks had probably been a member, organised at the Assembly Rooms in 1826. By this time in the period of the Regency the balls at the Assembly Rooms had become more glamorous with great attention being given to decorating the Rooms. The following year

The York Club Grand Masqued Fete, Upper Assembly Rooms, 1826

The doors were opened at 9 o'clock and the unmasked stewards, including General Sir Henry Johnson, welcomed the guests, The Octagon had been converted

> into a magnificent circular tent formed of crimson and white calico in bold stripes, the four entrances were characteristically ornamented, the floor was carpeted with crimson cloth and ottomans were judiciously disposed around: above the entrances waved silken banners; on either side stood pedestals encrusted with armour and warlike trophies, bearing antique massive candelabras; and the whole apartment presented a most novel and splendid *coup d'oeil.*

The ballroom was decorated for the supper buffet and was presented as an illuminated garden. The 103ft long room was laid out with a leafy central avenue with Chinese lanthorns along its length; at one end was a 40ft high Chinese pagoda wherein was 'the presiding *Joss* Selway who was dispensing 'cates of the choicest description'. At the other end of the avenue was a shrubbery with a glimpse of a further avenue beyond, an illusion created by a large mirror. Running along the centre of the avenue there were orange trees laden with 'golden fruit' and plinths on which were statues, including a cupid who was aiming arrows at the guests as they entered the room. On either side of the avenue, behind parterres of painted flowers and a low Chinese paling, were tables and attendants dispensing refreshments. The Card Room floor was painted in coloured chalks; it was a Regency fashion to chalk an elaborate design on a dance floor that would be danced away by the revellers over the course of an evening. One end was fitted with an orchestra occupied by the 'celebrated Pandean Band' who played pan pipes and percussion instruments; at the other end was Mr Grey's Fantoccini Theatre puppet show that 'performed to the very life and greatly amused the Company'. The dancing took place in the Tea Room that was chalked in Quadrille sets and there was a 'full band' in the orchestra. Among the many guests in fancy dress was Mr Heneage Gibbes, the son of Dr Gibbes the Franks' doctor when they visited Bath, who went as 'Ramo Samee the Indian Juggler', a popular conjurer and magician from India who had recently performed in the city. David Haliburton Dallas went as 'a West Indian slave imploring mercy'.

1827 Johnson was introduced to HRH the Duchess of Clarence when she visited Bath. He always donated to charitable causes including in 1822 a fund to cleanse and sanitise the poor and dirty parts of the city. General Sir Henry Johnson died at Catherine Place on the 18th March 1835 and was buried with Rebecca in St Michael's graveyard. A memorial to him was placed in the Abbey by the Bath Knot of Friendly Brothers of St Patrick – a social association formed in Dublin in the 1750s initially in an attempt to replace duelling with mediation.

The memorial to General Sir Henry Friendly Johnson in Bath Abbey: author's collection.

WHAT WERE JACOB AND PRISCILLA FRANKS LIKE?

THE CASH BOOK on which this book is based is catalogued in the London Metropolitan Archives as Priscilla's. All the internal evidence however suggests it was Jacob's. It records many of their joint activities but Priscilla drew her own funds from the budget covered by the book and how she spent that is not known. Neither is it known for certain whether many of the activities recorded – taking the hot mineral water cure, theatre going, concert going – were jointly enjoyed by both Franks or whether each had their own preferences. I have surmised in the book that it was Jacob who took the cure but this is not certain, on the other activities I have assumed that Priscilla and Jacob acted in concert.

A character portrait of Jacob Franks can be drawn from the cash book, assuming it was his, and other surviving evidence. When he journeyed to Britain as a young man his sister said of him 'he will be a feast [to his uncle Naphtali (Heartsey) Franks] as a pure exotick, he appears to be a pretty modest Young Fellow'.[234] The account book attests he was careful, meticulous and possibly obsessive. He kept and used the same account book for fifty years and included in it quotidian detail that normally would only have concerned the mistress of a household. These traits did not prevent him being friendly and sociable, he was clubbable and enjoyed public social occasions, he sought out people to meet when he was touring Britain and he sent his friends presents of his favourite cheese from Minifee the cheese monger.

Was Jacob Franks' attendance at plays and concerts an aspect of his sociability rather than a love of culture? There is no mention of bookshops or buying books (except directories and almanacks and one literary work - Tristram Shandy). They did subscribe to libraries (though on some visits only Priscilla did) and this was probably as much for their role as local information hubs where you could read the newspapers, find out where lodgings were available and buy tickets for balls and concerts, as much as to borrow books for leisure reading. This all suggests that the Franks were not part of the literary set in Bath that was centred around Lady Miller of Batheaston Villa and her poetical soirees in the late eighteenth century. One of either Jacob or Priscilla was a more frequent playgoer than the other; my intuitive assessment of the details in the cash book is that Priscilla was the one who enjoyed theatre more.

Jacob was probably hypochondriacal and always concerned with his health. Oddly there is no direct reference in the account book to either him or Priscilla taking – that is drinking – the Bath mineral water, only bathing and pumping. Perhaps the soda water that was frequently mentioned in the 1800s was carbonated Bath mineral water, a bottled product that was widely available.

234 Stern, op cit, p.92.

Jacob Franks' business style can be discerned in his correspondence about Duckenfield Hall. He was focussed on profitability and cutting costs as much as possible and he fixated on detail, to the irritation of his plantation attorney John Kelly who nevertheless tried hard to disguise it. In practice distance and the slowness of the mail made such forensic management by Jacob almost impossible.

The enslaved people on Duckenfield estate received no charitable concern from Jacob Franks. Equally when Priscilla owned the estate alone she seemed at ease with the institution of slavery. In all likelihood she and Jacob would have believed a fiction, never having visited the plantation, that they were benign and protective slave owners. Such a belief must have been hard to maintain through years when the anti-slavery movement was becoming more vociferous and urgent.

However Jacob and Priscilla were charitable towards their family and beyond. They were supportive of their wider family of siblings, nephews, nieces, great-nephews and great-nieces. In 1778 for example random notes on the front fly-leaf of the cash book reveal that two sword hilts had been bought, 'box and carriage paid' for 'Mrs Franks of Teddington', Priscilla Franks' sister Phila whose house was at Teddington, (were these gifts for her husband Moses, Jacob's uncle)? At about the same time Jacob gave money to his brother Moses and also loaned money to 'Abby'.

Support may often have been needed as the family dealt with scandal, such as the Cooper/Cadogan affair and with early death such as that of Captain George Pigot Johnson in the Peninsular War in 1812. Sometimes the Franks' efforts were perhaps to maintain the family's wealth rather than support a family member. Moses Franks died intestate in April 1789 and his widow Phila, Priscilla's sister, became a wealthy woman. The following month a jury of 'honest and lawful men of Middlesex' were convened at Phila's house in Teddington to take an inquisition of lunacy. They listed Phila's property and declared on oath that she was a lunatic and of unsound mind though she did 'enjoy lucid intervals'.[235] She was therefore unable to 'govern herself' or manage her property. They also added that she had been a lunatic since the 12th April 1788, the year before, but they did not know what caused her to become lunatic unless it were by 'visitation of God'.[236] Phila Franks' only child was Isabella Bell Cooper who was only twenty years old at that time and her

235   Phila Franks of Teddington Commission & Inquisition of Lunacy into her State of Mind and Property, National Archives, C211/9/F56.

236   Court of Chancery pleadings; Franks v Adolphus, National Archives C11/1683/21.

husband William Cooper became responsible for managing Phila's estate. It is not known what happened to Phila Franks after being declared lunatic but she was probably looked after by the family and she died in 1801 at her daughters home, Little Thurlow Hall in Suffolk.[237] Was Phila truly insane or had the family had her so declared to maintain family control of Moses' wealth?

The Franks were generous to charitable causes; there are frequent random charitable donations in the cash book – a poor soldier's wife, a street urchin boy, a waiter at the Rooms in hard times – and if the newspaper account is to be believed when the wealthy Judith Levy died intestate, leaving her domestic staff unprovided for, the Franks gave £1,000 to the butler and provision to the other servants in proportion. Jacob's behaviour to his own servants was benign. Priscilla Franks was also remembered in Isleworth for her charity and support of the poor.

Priscilla Franks' character is harder to discern but there are hints that she was an independent person. She clearly had her own money before she was widowed that she spent as she wished. The cash book she kept in her later years shows she was as meticulous in her financial affairs as her husband had been. There is a fleeting glimpse of her enjoying an independent outing around Lansdown in her own gig. Her will suggests that like Jacob she was a charitable person within her locality and much focussed on family; they were a family that needed to support each other as they had made a no doubt difficult social transition from Judaism to Christianity.

The world that Jane Austen evokes in her novels, visits to Bath, touring the north country, visiting the seaside, balls, concerts, patronising Molland's the confectioners of Milson Street, as did Austen's characters in 'Persuasion', and a focus on the tribulations of family life, all funded on wealth from the colonies, is very much the life that Jacob and Priscila Franks lived. And like Jane Austen herself they had a liminal life, close enough to the highest ranks of society to observe them but not quite close enough to be fully part of them, in their case because of the Jewish ancestry and in Jane Austen's case because of her lack of wealth.

237 *Oracle & Daily Advertiser*, 13/1/180, p.4a.

APPENDIX 1: THE FAMILY CONNECTIONS OF JACOB & PRISCILLA FRANKS[1]

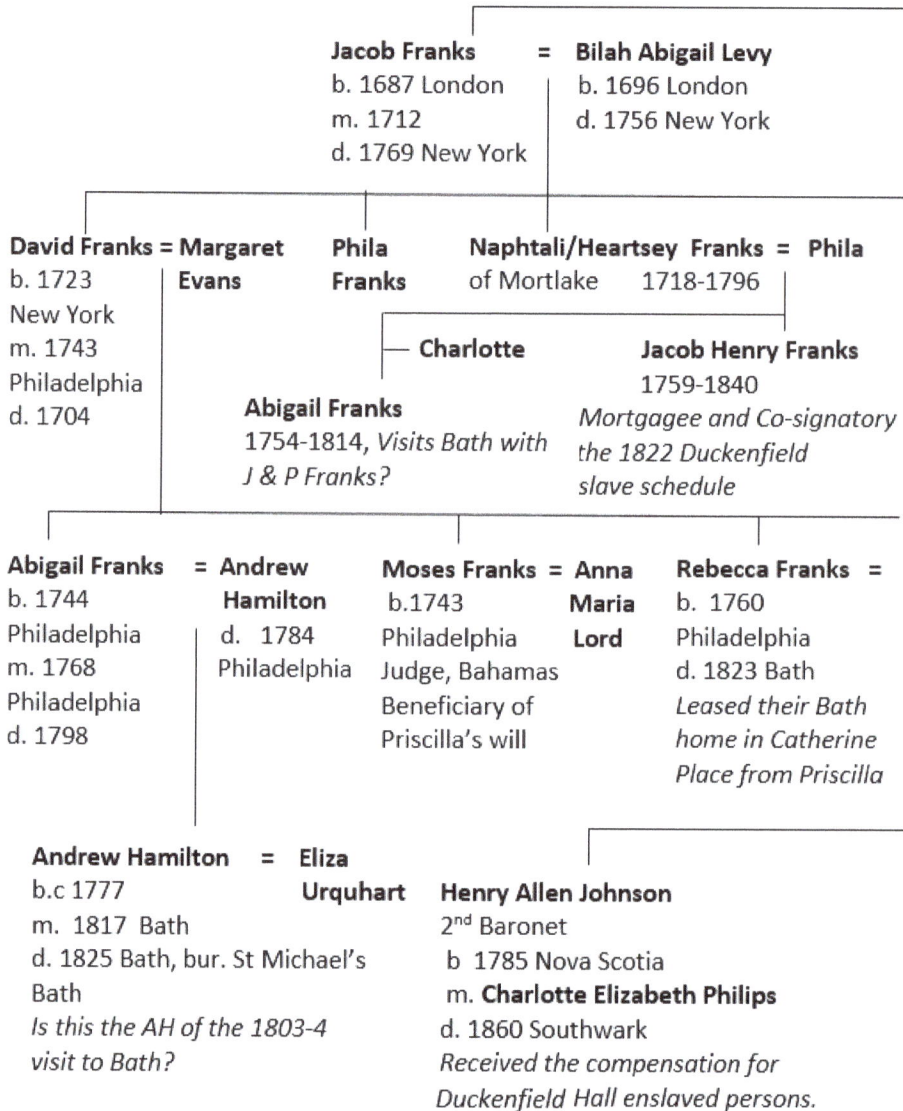

Jacob Franks   =   **Bilah Abigail Levy**
b. 1687 London   b. 1696 London
m. 1712   d. 1756 New York
d. 1769 New York

David Franks = Margaret   **Phila**   **Naphtali/Heartsey Franks = Phila**
b. 1723   **Evans**   **Franks**   of Mortlake   1718-1796
New York
m. 1743   — **Charlotte**   **Jacob Henry Franks**
Philadelphia   1759-1840
d. 1704   **Abigail Franks**   *Mortgagee and Co-signatory*
          1754-1814, *Visits Bath with*   *the 1822 Duckenfield*
          J & P Franks?   *slave schedule*

Abigail Franks   = **Andrew**   **Moses Franks = Anna**   **Rebecca Franks**   =
b. 1744   **Hamilton**   b.1743   **Maria**   b. 1760
Philadelphia   d. 1784   Philadelphia   **Lord**   Philadelphia
m. 1768   Philadelphia   Judge, Bahamas   d. 1823 Bath
Philadelphia   Beneficiary of   *Leased their Bath*
d. 1798   Priscilla's will   *home in Catherine*
                                                 Place from Priscilla

Andrew Hamilton   =   **Eliza**
b.c 1777   **Urquhart**   **Henry Allen Johnson**
m. 1817 Bath   2nd Baronet
d. 1825 Bath, bur. St Michael's   b 1785 Nova Scotia
Bath   m. **Charlotte Elizabeth Philips**
Is this the AH of the 1803-4   d. 1860 Southwark
visit to Bath?   *Received the compensation for*
                              Duckenfield Hall enslaved persons.

1   Stern, M. A. (1991) *First American Jewish Families*, p.75 & Ancestry.co.uk.

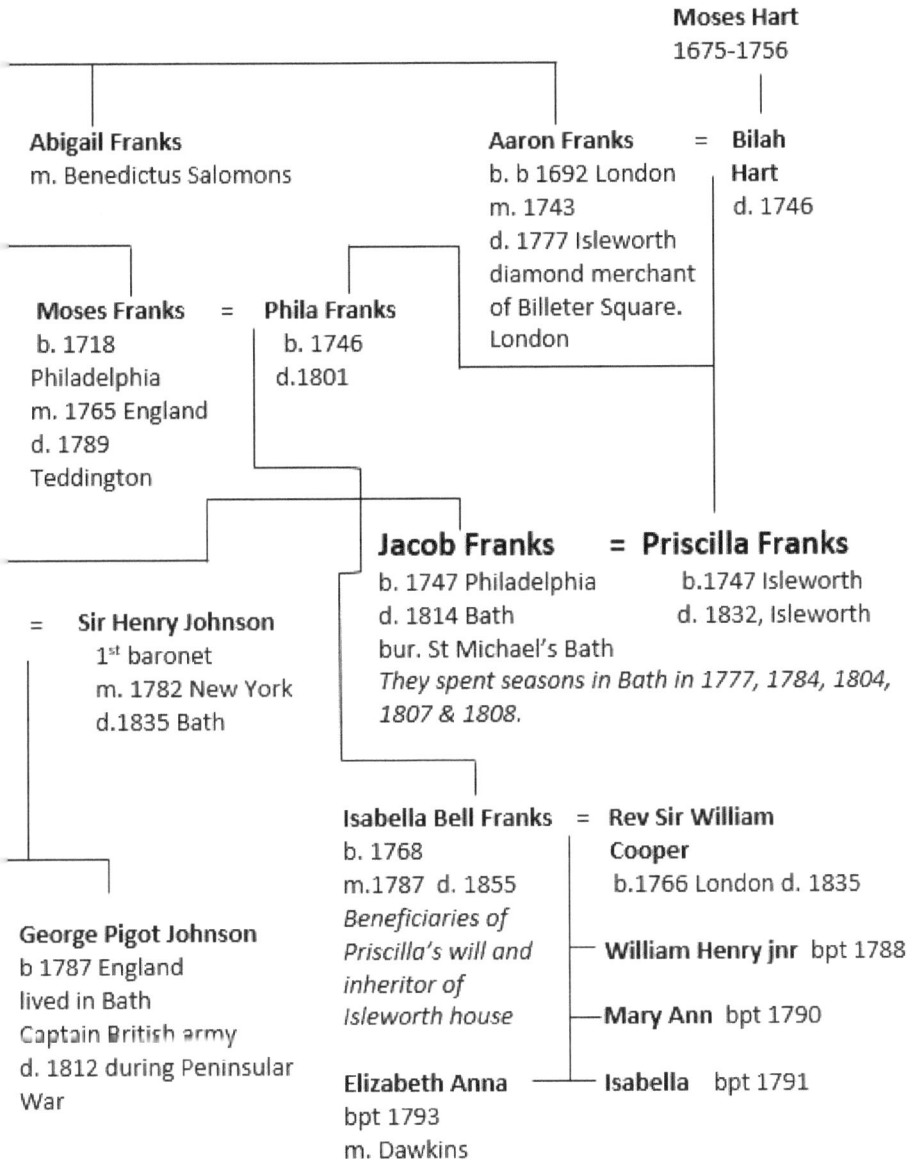

Moses Hart
1675-1756

Abigail Franks
m. Benedictus Salomons

Aaron Franks   =   **Bilah**
b. b 1692 London   **Hart**
m. 1743   d. 1746
d. 1777 Isleworth
diamond merchant
of Billeter Square.
London

Moses Franks   =   **Phila Franks**
b. 1718   b. 1746
Philadelphia   d.1801
m. 1765 England
d. 1789
Teddington

Jacob Franks   =   **Priscilla Franks**
b. 1747 Philadelphia   b.1747 Isleworth
d. 1814 Bath   d. 1832, Isleworth
bur. St Michael's Bath
They spent seasons in Bath in 1777, 1784, 1804,
1807 & 1808.

=   **Sir Henry Johnson**
       1st baronet
       m. 1782 New York
       d.1835 Bath

Isabella Bell Franks   =   **Rev Sir William**
b. 1768   **Cooper**
m.1787 d. 1855   b.1766 London d. 1835
Beneficiaries of
Priscilla's will and   —   **William Henry jnr** bpt 1788
inheritor of
Isleworth house   ——**Mary Ann** bpt 1790

George Pigot Johnson
b 1787 England
lived in Bath
Captain British army   —   **Isabella**   bpt 1791
d. 1812 during Peninsular
War   **Elizabeth Anna**   ——
                            bpt 1793
                            m. Dawkins

APPENDIX 2: A GLOSSARY OF EIGHTEENTH CENTURY TERMS & SLANG

Bath Brick	'Bath Brick is made near Bridgwater. It is a substance, used for polishing or cleaning metallic utensils, consisting of a fine Silicious Sand deposit in the River Parret near that town. The substance is called Bath Brick, because it was and is so largely used in that town'. Peach, R.E.M. Street Lore of Bath p.154.
bath or bathing chairs	See 'Chairs and chairmen'.
Bath wigs	Wigs were a breakfast bun served in wedge shapes and flavoured with caraway seeds. Charlotte Mason The Lady's Assistant for Regulating and supplying the table (1801). For Bath Wigs see Bath Chronicle 16/6//1928, p.4. also Peach Street Lore of Bath, p. 152.
Beetela cambrick	A fine and thin white muslin textile from India.
blister / blistering	A medical treatment involving applying a plaster coated in an irritant to the skin that causes a blister that is then drained.
breeches ball	A soap -like cake used for covering marks and stains on men's breeches. Also known as yellow ball. There were various recipes with various ingredients such as kaolin, Bath Brick, ox galls and ochre.
brim	Slang: an abandoned and irascible woman (Francis Grosse, The Vulgar Tongue), and by extension something that had lost its value.
bulse	A purse or bag to carry precious stones, from the Portuguese, bolsa – bag.
Chairs and chairmen	An enclosed chair for one person carried on poles by two men known as chairmen. The bathing chair and its successor the close chair were for carrying people to and from their bedrooms to the hot mineral baths. They were consequently lighter and smaller than the Sedan chair which was constructed of wood and leather and had glass windows. The Sedan chairs was used for general transport around the city and was carried on long poles which gave the chair some bounce as the chairmen carried it over the uneven pavements. The bathing chairs were carried on short poles so they could be taken into houses and carried up to bedrooms where the client would be wrapped in blankets and put in the chair to be taken to the baths.

Close chairs	See 'Chairs and chairmen'.
clyster	An enema or suppository.
coques	A small loop of ribbon used for trimming and for hat making.
cotillion	The cotillion was a French country square dance involving four partners that had become popular in the 1760s. Cotillion balls were probably less formal than the Dress Balls at which the intricate and stately minuet was danced.
Court plaisters	These were beauty patches for the face much used in the eighteenth century. They were made from strips of satin coated on one side with a mixture of isinglass and glucose. Sometimes they were used medically.
cupping	A treatment for sciatica and muscle pain; a heated glass vessel was placed over the skin creating a vacuum as it cooled it drew the skin into the vessel.
dangle, dangler	To hang after or about a person, especially as a loosely attached follower; to follow in a dallying way, without being a formally recognised attendant (Oxford English Dictionary.) Dangler —one who follows women in general without any particular attachment, Grose, Francis, The Vulgar Tongue.
diavolinos	A confectionery; sugar balls flavoured with chocolate or peppermint.
diligence	A four wheeled enclosed coach used for long journeys.
douters	Rods with a cone at the end used for extinguishing candles.
false tail	Gentlemen's wigs had a short pony tail known as a queue at the back, a false tail was a queue on a piece of thin string that could be tied around the head under a hat. (qv queue)
fantoccini	Puppets operated by hand from above; travelling fantoccini puppet shows first arrived in Britain from Italy in about 1770 and rapidly became popular entertainments.
Gattie's Esprit de Rose	A perfume or eau d'toilette.
gig	A light two wheeled, sprung vehicle drawn by one horse; also known as a chaise.
gloves	A small bribe, a commission payment, to encourage someone to provide a service. The Oxford English Dictionary gives 'a pair of gloves' to mean a pretext for making a gift of money, nominally intended to buy gloves with.

Gourlard Extract	A patent medicine for inflammation.
Gouty chairs	Pushchairs for invalids and people suffering from gout. They were sometimes known as Merlin chairs after John. Joseph Merlin the inventor of a self-propelling invalid chair
Hart's Horn	Shavings of hartshorn were used in the kitchen as a setting agent to make jellies.
Hautboy	An old name for an oboe.
Ho'ryean	Ho' bryean (Chateau Haut Brion) claret imported from Bordeaux.
isinglass	A gelling or setting agent derived from whales and fish.
limner	A painter and portraitist.
Lisbon, a bottle of,	Portuguese white wine.
Madeira buns	Specialist buns made in Bath to go with Madeira wine.
mephitic air	Carbon dioxide.
mocho / mocha	An agate or chalcedony stone used in jewellery.
negus	A mulled wine diluted with water and flavoured with sugar and nutmeg.
Opodeldec	An alcohol based liniment to treat inflammation often including laudanum.
orgeat (orzyat)	An almond syrup cordial.
oznaburg	A cheap coarse textile originally made from flax that was used to provide clothing for enslaved people on sugar plantations.
pamboxes	Not listed in any dictionary, at a guess it could relate to the card game of pam or five card loo as a box to store the playing cards in.
pattens	A shoe or clog with a raised sole, or set on an iron ring, to keep feet out of the wet and the mud.
pelisse	A long cloak often lined with fur.
pennistone	A cheap, coarse woollen cloth dyed blue exported to the West Indies to provide clothing for enslaved people on the plantations. It was known as 'negro cloth' or 'slave cloth'.
Pew opener	An attendant at a church or chapel who escorted you to your pew, which sometimes had a small gate at the aisle end, and who expected a tip.
pigeon	Card cheats' slang term for their victim or mark.

pinchbeck	An alloy of copper and zinc used to imitate gold in jewellery. Invented by Christopher Pinchbeck, father of the Mr Pinchbeck who owned the Tunbridge Wells Assembly Rooms.
ridotto	A public social assembly with music and dancing.
rout	A private party held at home for cards and gossip.
queue	The pony tail attached to the rear of a gentleman's wig, from the French for tail; (qv false tail).
Sedan chairs	See 'Chairs and chairmen'.
sharper	A card cheat, normally part of a gang who would groom a mark, cheat them and then demand satisfaction at a duel if the mark did not pay up.
Sharpers' ball	Not listed in any dictionary, at a guess this is Jacob Franks' satirical name for a masquerade ball. Or perhaps it is an obsolete term for something not at all connected to dancing?
spermaceti	Whale oil used to make the most expensive type of candle.
spruce beer	A beer introduced from America that was made with the buds and tips of the spruce tree and molasses.
square plait	An embroidery stich and knot pattern.
ton	Stylish, elegant and exclusive, from the French bon-ton. 'The ton' means an exclusive and superior social set.
toy, toyshop, toyman	A toy was a fancy good for adults, such as snuff boxes, jewellery, trinkets and it was sold in toyshops by toymen of whom there were many in eighteenth century Bath.
vails	A tip to a servant for providing the cards and candles during a rout.
Wafer seals	These were used instead of wax to seal letter. A dough of flour, egg white, isinglass and yeast was made, rolled out and baked and cut into round wafers. They would be licked and used to seal a letter.
Warner's Milk of Roses	A patent skin cream.
Water Souché [souchey].	A dish of fresh water fish poached and served in a broth, introduced to England from the Netherlands.
yaws	Yaws is a skin infection spread by skin contact that was endemic in West Indian plantations in the nineteenth century.

Appendix 3: Indecipherables & Cryptics

Images courtesy of the London Metropolitan Archives.

The handwriting in the Franks' cash book is mostly neat and clear but it was a private note book not written to be read by others and so sometimes the writing is a little lazy and the letters not discernible and at other times a note is made that meant something to the writer but is too cryptic to be understood by others. So when reading a historical document such as the cash book sometimes a judgement, or more accurately an intuitive leap, is required, and sometimes these can be wrong. I have put a few examples below so that the reader can see how using old documents is not straightforward; and in the hope that perhaps someone can make more sense of the words than I can!

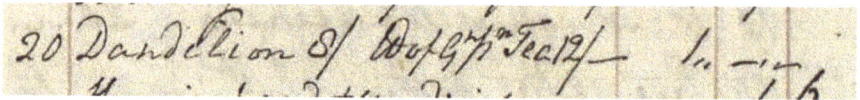

Entrance to Dandelion cost 8s., tea was expensive - 12s so what was the other initialled item before the word 'tea'?

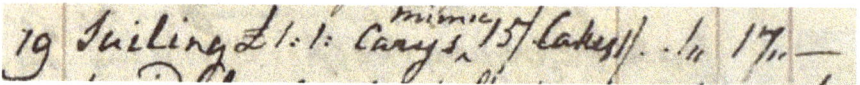

What is Carys mimic – if that is what it says, costing 15/-? (Possibly Cary's Itinerary, *a guidebook for travellers in Britain).*

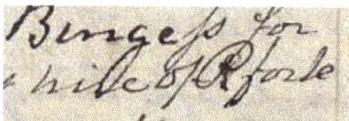

What was hired from Mr Burgess?

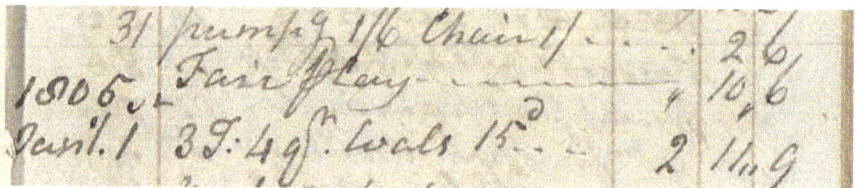

What, who or why is Fair Play?

Does this entry refer to a Marquis St Leger? (20th February 1805)

What did he buy a pair of? (27th May 1805)

What is the second item on the bill – 'airing toll'? 26th May 1806, Clifton.

What was being carried? 8th December 1804.

What was the payment of £25 to Durand on the 26th December 1804 for?

PICTURE CREDITS

Akeman Press
Alamy
Author's collection
Bath in Time
Bath Record Office
British Museum
Jewish Museum, London
Leicestershire Record Office
Lewis Walpole Library, Yale University
Lost Pubs Project
London Metropolitan Archives
Look & Learn Picture Collection
Michael Birkett-Jones
Michael's Bookshop, Ramsgate
Royal Academy of Arts
Yale Center for British Art: Paul Mellon Collection

I have been unable to identify the copyright owner of images nos. 4 & 5 and would be willing to make appropriate acknowledgements should they become known.

ACKNOWLEDGEMENTS

Thanks to Tatjana LeBoff and Tim Moore, Project Curators at the National Trust's Assembly Rooms at Bath; this book began as a research profile I produced as a volunteer researcher for the National Trust and they have both been supportive of my eighteenth century delvings. Many thanks also to Andrew Swift, Michael Birkett-Jones and Anne Buchanan for their help. The Hobnob Press run by John Chandler and Louise Ryland-Epton have made the publication of this book possible and particular thanks to John for the attractive design of the book. The Hobnob Press provide an essential outlet for people who want to make their local history projects easily accessible and John and Louise deserve thanks for making it successful.

INDEX

www.ingramcontent.com/pod-product-compliance
Lightning Source LLC
Chambersburg PA
CBHW051211090426
42740CB00022B/3463